OVERCOMING ALL ODDS THREE

What Students Taught Me

Ron N. Reel Ph.D.

FOREWORD TO BOOK THREE

In the first book of my autobiography, I told my story from birth through departing to go to Bethany Bible College. Book One showed how I survived poverty, several serious illnesses, and physical and emotional abuse from my father. I needed help from a loving mother, facilitative teachers, encouraging clergy and their congregations, and a number of friends I made along the way.

In Book Two, I told what happened to me between the summer of 1968 through the summer of 1974, discussing the four colleges I attended and noting the unique challenges each of them provided. I had to overcome academic and personal challenges, including accusations of plagiarism, negative stereotyping from several professors, too much alcohol consumption, and my own lack of self-confidence. Together they resulted in a bout of acute depression and even my consideration of suicide.

I described the various jobs I undertook to pay for my college education. Once again, God sent teachers and friends to help me overcome all obstacles and to keep my college education on track. My intent was to encourage anyone reading my books to defeat their own demons and to help others overcome similar obstacles.

In this third volume I will share problems I faced as a beginning teacher with parents, administrators, fellow faculty, staff, competitor coaches, faculty union issues and academic senate challenges, and how both my students and I overcame minor and major obstacles that certainly changed our lives.

Some of the problems were academic, some financial, and some religious in nature. At one point, I found myself teaching at a private religious institution combining academic and church related issues. My own public education had prepared me for challenges found there, but I was left doubting myself in certain aspects unique to private schooling and the religious aspects of new rules, regulations, and curriculum acceptable in that type of school.

In this memoir I have changed the location and names of schools as well as the names of all the people but two. I have done my best to hide the identity of people I met along the way. Should similarities arise, it is only coincidental and no one person should assume they are that person. In fact, to make the narrative easier to follow, in a few situations, I have combined the actions of two or more different people into the actions of one.

Through it all, I felt the backing and support of family, friends, and allies who became my family. Once again, God brought people to help me out of the worst hours and allowed me to enjoy a new life filled with love and forgiveness for those who did me wrong, and comfort and caring for those that stepped up to help show the way.

I wish to thank John Arrijuria for proofreading this volume and pointing out suggestions that needed to be addressed in a better light than when I first wrote it. He also pointed out small things that needed some attention. I have come to rely on his expertise.

I also wish to thank Dr. Hal Bochin, not only for being the major editor, but for being my writing coach. His contributions, suggestions, advice, and mostly his friendship allowed me to complete this project. He taught me, and because of him, I have been blessed.

CHAPTER ONE: BAKERSFIELD COLLEGE

Todd Ledecki

I was proud of the fact I was the youngest professor ever hired at Bakersfield Junior College to a tenure track position. At the job interview I was told I was exactly what they wanted. I spent my first two weeks canvassing what seemed like the entire campus searching for any student wanting to join the speech team.

I left messages on all the poster board sites on campus. I met with the student activities director, an older woman, who told me to try to recruit athletes, nurses, and drama students because they seemed to have some time and a lot of talent.

None I met wanted to take on any additional responsibilities. I asked her about the students in student government. She informed me that I should recruit the officers of the student body if I wanted motivated students who were responsible for the funding for student activities. At the same time, she warned me that the current group of ASB officers were carrying too many classes, involved in too many causes, and had too many meetings! She felt they had too much going on to do anything else. In fact, she informed me that most could barely meet their academic obligations and keep their mandatory course load and grades high enough to stay in their office semester by semester. All the time and energy I gave seemed hopeless in my pursuit of students I could mold into winners.

I then asked permission of each of the beginning public speaking class professors to allow me to pitch my program in their classes and made my way through fifteen classes. Each professor allowed me five minutes to make a presentation. Many of the professors when introducing me would foreshadow what I was going to speak about with their own commentary about how much work would be involved in addition to what they were already doing in their own class. A few of those students met with me, but none showed much interest when I explained the commitment I wanted from them, and the travel that would be necessary to attend various tournaments. None seemed to have any interest in doing what was needed to be a winner, and some wanted not even to be held accountable for doing just enough to pass. Forensics would not be part of their college course education.

I was sitting in my office feeling a little dejected and unappreciated while I was preparing to go to my first evening Public Speaking class, located in my hometown of Wasco (about twenty-five miles from campus). It was the second week of on campus classes but for some reason, it was the first week for the classes at that location. I was hoping to have all my students on the same page at the same time each week. It would be challenging to be a week behind for this class.

A tall slender young man approached my office.

I hoped he wanted to enroll in my forensics course, but I quickly changed direction when I found myself thinking he was probably just seeking directions to a classroom next door or two doors away from my office.

"Are you Mr. Reel?" he asked.

"I am he!" I said, smiling.

"My name is Todd Ledecki, and I was a debater and individual events competitor at Bakersfield South High School," he said. I had done my homework researching the nearby high schools and knew that Bakersfield South was the powerhouse school in the entire valley.

"Those are some impressive credentials if you in fact did both debate and speech," I said, searching for more clarification as to exactly what Todd had done and to find out how successful he had been.

"I wasn't at the top of the class in debate because of who I was; and my parents did not have enough money to contribute to after school activities. I know how to talk because I have been doing that since I was about one. I am damn good if I do say so myself. My real interest is in interpretation of oral literature; especially retelling stories from novels," he said, smiling again. He paused to see if that statement was going to get a reaction. "Did you do anything else besides forensics in high school?"

"I went to the valley championship in swimming my junior and senior years," he said proudly. He proceeded to walk into my office and sat down in the empty chair.

"Diving or sprints?" I asked.

"Both! Valley finalist in the 100 and placed 5th in platform diving," he bragged.

"I must leave soon to drive to my night class out in Wasco. Do you know how far it is from the college? I start a public speaking class there tonight," I shared looking at my watch.

"It should take the average driver around thirty-five minutes. I can probably get you there closer to twenty-five minutes," Todd claimed with a big smile on his face. He seemed so confident and different from the few students I had met previously. His confidence was refreshing. I wanted to stay and discuss his future goals to become more familiar with whom I was meeting. He seemed to be candid. I liked him.

"I will take the slower route and know I will arrive in one piece." I continued gathering materials needed for the first night of class.

"I am sure the first night won't be more than twenty or so minutes, so, if you like, I can take you and wait for your class to get over so we can continue to talk about my future in competitive public speaking. If you don't want me to take you, perhaps, we can set an appointment for tomorrow when you are available to evaluate my chances to become the best speaker, I know I can become. I hear you need people, which I think means you have not formed any preconceived notions about who has money, family ties, or community status that gives an edge when it comes to getting help from you. You want a chauffeur for tonight?" Todd questioned again and smiled as he stood up.

"I think I will pass for tonight, but I am sure we will have many more opportunities to drive places together. Let's meet tomorrow at noon here in my office. One thing you can do for me before our meeting tomorrow is to put together a list of students you know that are here at the college who have had forensics experience. I don't care how much experience. In fact, if they have little or none, I can teach them without any bad habits already present because of some other coach or teacher. Let me have a list of whom I might contact to see if they want to join a team that will provide them with the opportunity to learn, win, and have a lot of fun," I said smiling and moving toward the door.

"I know several people who have experience in oratory and informative speaking, a couple impromptu and extemporaneous speakers, and two misfits who would make a great debate team for starters," he declared.

I wanted to stay and get to the bottom of this last statement but knew it would take too long and I could not be late for class. As I walked toward the door with my briefcase full and my hopes for a great first-class meeting, I knew that tomorrow would bring the beginning of a wonderful experience of student involvement and a chance to change the lives of those willing to work hard and seek more than what they thought possible. It would be an opportunity for others to move from the fields to become whatever they desired.

I wanted to be a part of their new journey. Their journey would teach me many things about other people who sometimes looked like me, but other times they had very little resemblance to me nor my world.

My posted office hours started at 12:00 p.m. the next day. As I opened the door to my office, Todd was already inside seated in the same chair he had sat in the night before!

"I like a person who is punctual," he said as he started whistling the song, *It's Off to Work I Go.*

"I too like people who are punctual. I won't even ask how you got into my office. Don't tell me if you broke in because I would have to report you to the campus police if you broke in like a criminal. Did you break into this well-equipped office housing the next great forensics coach?"

"I did....not. It was open."

"I am assuming you completed your homework assignment and have some names for me, don't you?" I asked walking to my desk.

"I did, but first I would like to share with you why I chose to attend this junior college." he said, placing a chair directly in front of where I was sitting.

"I imagine you chose this school because you heard I was here now and would provide the training for those who want to challenge themselves to the highest level." I hoped he knew I was joking but I meant every word I said.

"I was never quite good enough to be at the top level of anything I did. I could not get enough coaching for debate and individual events because of the tradition of elitism at my old school where parents demanded that their child be heard, tutored, given opportunities not available to everyone. Those students got more attention than they deserved. Every time I was ready to move to the top two or three teams in debate, a new or wealthier student arrived with a parent who were much pushier than mine." Todd claimed.

"Why didn't you go to your coach and share your feelings? It doesn't appear you have any problem disclosing how you feel," I said, seeking some type of reasoning behind this information being presented early in our relationship.

"I have much more confidence today than I had then. I have been out of high school for four years and have had time to reflect on what took place then and now know I can be as good as I choose; of course, with the help of someone of your caliber," Todd smiled and stopped talking to see if I would respond.

"I am sorry you ever felt inferior or overlooked. I promise you that will never happen in our relationship. You can expect the truth, assistance, and support. You will be challenged and only you will make the determination of how much contribution of effort you decide is the right amount.

I will place you in events and contests that will find you winning some and losing in other competitions early in the semester. You must lose to the best, those better than you, to become the best. You will learn from every competitor you face. I will push, suggest, help revise, and develop strategies that you may use; but it will be up to you, the judges, the competition you face, and your readiness that will ultimately determine how far you will go. Does that sound like something you want to try? Forensics is not like a track race where the fastest person wins automatically. You must convince each judge why you should be voted number one. They must like you and want you to win! You must persuade them with your demeanor, kindness to fellow competitors, preparedness, and even what you wear. I imagine you have several suits. You must learn to dress the part of a great speaker. You must look like the part you want them to see. Survey after survey suggests that when two people of equal quality perform in speech, the one dressed the best usually scores higher over the other person. You and I will have to make sure you are dressed expertly with just enough style that says professional but not pretentious.

Does that sound like something you want to try?" I asked.

"I just want someone to believe in me. I can be a winner. I am almost to the point where I want to be by believing in myself. I need someone to believe in me. All I have ever wanted to happen is to be given an equal opportunity to succeed and to have the playing field the same for all participants. If you are my coach and I do what you suggest I may become a national champion. I will have the same opportunity to win as anyone representing any college or university!" Todd declared, looking, and feeling liberated. I did not want to lessen his enthusiasm nor his desire to succeed.

"I don't know if that will ever happen if you join our team because we are at a junior college. Some judges at the university level will demand much more of you because in their minds a junior college student is automatically inferior. It will become our mission to allow those who hear you to feel they are listening to the best student from any college; four years or two years. I will work harder, longer, and prepare you better than any other coach if you allow me to have you as my student. Together we can overcome the junior college stigma," I promised. I had done it myself and knew in my heart it could be done again!

I felt I was going back in time and seeing myself but this time I was the teacher who hopefully would make the difference for this student. I knew the hunger he had to succeed was the same as what I had so many years earlier when I was in Shafter High School.

"I think we should start preparing me for a run for the "Gold" awards this week. My fiancée will have to share me with you for the next two semesters," he suddenly announced. I wondered what his fiancée thought of his new endeavor. I wanted to meet someone who was planning a life with this soon to be star. I wanted him to tell me something about her.

"You want your fiancée to share you with me?"

"Of course. She is very giving."

"Before you get away, who are those other students that will compliment you as our team begins to grow in numbers and quality?" I asked.

As promised, Todd took out a typed sheet from his briefcase and handed it to me. The names of three girls and one boy were identified as individual events speakers. Terry Cummings and DeWayne Lessberry were labeled as "debaters." He did not make any promises concerning any of the named students.

It was interesting that Todd had not placed his name under the debate area of the note. One of the people had four stars listed in very large print. He quickly became a great storyteller. I needed Todd to help guide me in dealing with students that saw me as a colleague and friend instead of a professor.

Todd soon became a stable person for all of us.

He encouraged some to step out and try new events and new programs. He listened and critiqued like he was a coach. He was certainly the team's student coach. He also branched out in his events too. By the time we got to nationals he was doing oral interpretation of literature, poetry, informative speaking, Lincoln-Douglas debate, and was part of our Reader's Theatre production. His other program did not place.

Todd won national honors in oral interpretation of literature, Lincoln-Douglas Debate, and Reader's Theater. He left his fiancé when he met the woman of his dreams during his participation in forensics. They married, had two children, and Todd rose through the ranks within the Kern County Police Department and retired as the police department chief. In addition to his working full-time with the police department, he also coached the debate team at Delano College for ten years and they became a powerhouse college under his tutelage. He taught me to expect the best in people until they prove otherwise. He showed me what humility looks like during competition and outside of the forensics world. Todd taught me what is to be a man of his word.

CHAPTER TWO:
BAKERSFIELD COLLEGE

Terry Cummings and DeWayne Lessberry

Todd had promised me he would deliver two people who had debated at different high schools and had not liked each other much, but he felt would make a great team because they were so different and each one had unique skills the other did not possess.

He felt they would grow into a formidable team.

The first to arrive was Terry Cummings. He looked like he was about sixteen years old. He was thin, tall, had curly blond hair, and spoke with an unusual cadence and placed emphasis on certain words he wanted you to catch.

"Mr. Reel, I presume," he said. I was sitting at my desk, and I had placed a plaque on the outside of the door with my name attached.

"I am he!" I replied.

"I was told by an older student whom I didn't know when I was competing; but now know because he has judged me at local tournaments. He looks older than what I think a man his age should. I think it is his loss of hair. He said you were looking for debate people and I enjoyed it immensely for the two years I participated." he shared as he sat down in the (chair of stars) as I would soon call it.

"I am looking for students who want to win state and national honors. Are you one of those students?" I asked looking directly into his youthful face.

"Well, I think I would enjoy doing it. My mother did not let me advance much in competitive speaking because she felt I should spend my time on becoming a subject expert in higher level math and science," he said, smiling and waiting for me to ask why she directed him in a very specific area.

"Don't you think your mother should have asked if you wanted to pursue fields other than math and science?"

"I am sure she wanted what was best for me. She is quite disappointed I am here at this college instead of at a major university. She feels I need to be away at this time, and I insisted on remaining here at home." Terry said very proudly.

"I want you to be happy. Let's leave your mother alone for a minute or two and talk about you," I suggested.

"She has watched over me and planned my future since I was born. She is the principal of North Central High School and wants me to be one of those who leave Bakersfield and make something of themselves!" he said as he took a breath of fresh air.

"I think the important question is what do you want to happen with your life?" I pushed him to make his own decision.

"I was just getting known as a good debater when Mother thought I was spending too much time and effort in an area that would bring minimal reward. My grades and score on the SAT's got me offers from the schools she wanted me to attend. She was very disappointed when I did not agree to go to any of them. I don't know how she will respond because I still live in her home. I do know she would rather me stay at home than leave and not have some control," he said when a glow of self-discovery appeared in front of both of us.

"It seems to me you have decided to make a run at finding out how far you can advance in debate," I responded knowing for the first time in his life, he wanted to be his own person.

"Seems like you might be right. I know my mother, and she will always want what is best for me. She will need to understand she has raised a son who has listened and learned and can make good solid decisions regarding his life." Terry said smiling. He soon left my office to go to class.

Within twenty minutes after Terry left my office there was a knock at the door. The door was closed, and I could not see anyone.

"Please come in," I said in a slightly louder voice than usual. There was no movement or noise on the other side of the door. Again, there was a knock louder than the last.

"Mr. Reel are you holding office hours today?" came a loud, easily understandable voice.

"I am! Please enter!" I replied hoping it would be a new forensics student.

The door opened and a young man about 5' 6" tall, dark brown hair, thick black rimmed glasses, a sporadic mustache that one could not tell whether it was more than a few days old or belonged to someone who should not be sporting that look entered my office. He stood there looking disheveled and his first impression was not too confident.

"Hello, I am here to audition for your debate team. Todd suggested I audition for what he thinks will be a great forensics program and bring all of us who were misfits or overlooked in high school a chance to meet our potential." he said, pausing to hear and see my response.

"I don't know I would call this an audition. At this point I only have one other person interested in debate," I shared because I didn't want to start my relationship under false pretense.

"First, what is your name and, please tell me about your experience and yourself," I requested.

"I am DeWayne Lessberry, someday to be DeWayne Lessberry, Esquire. I graduated from North Bakersfield High School, and I have quite a bit of debate experience. Neither of my parents wanted me and so I have lived for the past three years at the orphanage here in town after my last foster parents said they could not afford to keep me. When a child turns eighteen, they term out and can no longer stay in the system and the child (me) must move out. I turned eighteen two weeks ago. The administrators like me and are trying to let me stay a few weeks longer, but I will be forced to be out on my own within a couple more months at best. I can go and get a few meals but cannot stay at night much longer. I wish I had a family, but I don't. I am sure I am not alone, and many others have faced the same situation. I must decide how to proceed," he said, telling his story so articulately and emotionally that I almost started crying there on the spot. I didn't know whether to believe him or not.

"Are you making this up to show how expressive and moving you can be, or are you legitimately sharing your life story?" I asked.

"I did just turn eighteen, and I am termed out of lodging, and because the orphanage can no longer collect funds on me, I was asked to leave," he said. I didn't know whether to be mad at the orphanage or the state of California that would do this to the youngest of adults.

"I don't remember your name after all the emotion that was shared. How do I help to get you some financial aid?" I asked now that I suddenly determined he was a frail, brave, and courageous young man.

"DeWayne is my name, but I really want to be known as DeWayne Debater Extraordinaire (DDE). I can present compelling, emotional, and reasoned arguments that will impact the smart, not so smart, and even those who are illogical. I can be very compelling while at the same time very competitive. People outside of the rounds will like me and my backstory. You and I can be a good partnership. Most of them won't be intimidated by me and will underestimate what I will be able to do. They will put down their guard. My dream partner would be someone who researches, sees the logical conclusion, but can share that knowledge with me to present it in a manner anyone can understand. He would be the first speaker on each side we have, and I would be the closer. You know the person that makes the final lasting impression. A person that will seal the deal.

Do you have anyone that might fit that bill?" he asked almost out of breath. Before I could respond, he continued.

"It would be better if he, or she, had a place where we both could reside so we could devote all our free time to research and perfecting arguments."

I knew by this time; I had the perfect match that miraculously had showed up and landed square in the Bakersfield College speaking field. Terry's mom loved the idea that Terry and Dewayne would share the garage bedroom Terry's parents had converted into a suite with kitchen and bath. I had to make sure I could have them stand out as superiors in dress that would match their superiority in presentation and debate. I took them to a clothing shop and bought them two matching suits. Their attire would help with the mystique I could create for them.

Early in the season, they had one judge from Claremont Community College who gave them a loss each time she judged them. They were making it to the final round in most of the tournaments, but when we got back and read the comments that judge provided, proved she did not like them for some unknown reason. She praised their logic used; but always found a reason not to vote for them. One Wednesday when we were practicing, Terry informed me about a plan of action they wanted me to mastermind.

"We all agree that this one judge consistently gives us a loss. She always manages to come to some type of weak reasoning to do so, but we have a plan that will prevent her from judging us." Terry said with a smile. DeWayne turned his head away and was no longer engaged in the conversation. It appeared he was hiding from what was going to be said next. I suddenly felt blindsided.

"We have done some research on her, and this is our assessment and course of action we need implemented." Dewayne interjected, as he turned back to face both of us.

"OK, what is it?" I asked.

"First, she is very attractive and is a professional college professor just like yourself," Terry stated.

"Second, her parents are quite wealthy. They put her through Claremont McKenna College according to sources we contacted (fellow debaters from her school)," DeWayne shared.

"Third, she is single and looking for a partner!" blurted out Terry.

"Finally, if she were to be dating you, she could not judge us because of a conflict that the two of you were an item!!" Dewayne said as he sat down for effect. Both boys really enjoyed this part of their plan. Their innocence and immaturity were showing. They must have rehearsed this scenario a couple times and waited for me to respond to their crazy plan. I thought I would have some fun with them for just a couple of minutes.

"Well, gentlemen, I do say I have not heard of

this type of approach to banning someone from judging a particular team before. I think it would be easier if I just hired a hit person and had her taken out. It will be quick, and you won't have to worry about her any longer. I have relatives that would do this for me. Besides, you don't even know if either of us like each other, so that way emotion won't get in the way of having it carried out, and you having to bail me out of jail," I said, wanting to get back to perhaps even a better job at debating instead of putting my personal life out there to keep a judge from doing what judges are supposed to do.

"Her debaters told us that she finds you very attractive and her nickname for you is 'Mr. Gold' because of your blonde hair," Terry said smiling from cheek to cheek.

"I can't believe she would share something like that with her students!" I said with great force; trying to hide some excitement about a potential interested female.

"We know almost everything about you too! Although we did not give any information about you to those two cute girl debaters," DeWayne said as he was blushing.

"I won't call any of my relatives to put a hit out on her. I want nothing said about me to any of her students. If I do decide to ask her out, it will be on my own terms. Have I made myself clear gentlemen?" I asked as convincingly as possible under those circumstances.

After she dropped them twice at the next tournament, I decided I should get to know her. I asked her out and we began dating.

CHAPTER THREE:
BAKERSFIELD COLLEGE

Caudie Brown

My public speaking class held in Wasco was producing some very interesting students. It was a mixture of students who had just graduated from high school, those raising young children, and over half the class were students who had retired and wanted to find something to do. I had asked the students on the first night of class to share why they had enrolled in the class, what they thought they would get out of the class, and the reason they thought now was the time to take public speaking.

Caudie Brown amazed me with her answers the first night. As she approached the front of the classroom, I could tell she was nervous because she was taking deep breaths, (she had a slight whistling sound) and she was gazing down at the floor each step of her way forward. When she turned to face the students and me, she paused, took one last breath, and began speaking.

"Good evening fellow classmates, my name is Caudie Brown and I live in Shafter, a small town just seven miles from here. I am going to answer the questions our professor has asked us in a slightly different order than he suggested. I have my own house cleaning business, and my husband, Billy, works for Shell Oil Company. I am a mother of four children (all grown), and I am taking this class, truth be told... I am here tonight... because I have done for others almost my entire life and it is now time for me to do something for me. I love to paint, and some have told me I am pretty damn good!

I have wanted to talk about all kinds of things with people before because I wanted to express how I felt but was told I could upset people around me if I had a different opinion from others felt I should have. So, I enrolled to make me a better person by learning how to say what I feel needs to be said in a way that makes me feel good, but also keeping in mind the person I am talking with might have other feelings that might be hurt if I am not considering their point of view.

After hearing the amazing story of how our professor, as young as he is, was able to come from this same valley and accomplish so much, I want to learn from each of you and him how to present facts, stories, and illustrations to the best of my ability. The reason this is the time for me to take this class is very personal. I gave up much of what I wanted to accomplish because I married very young, I had children to raise, and I put their lives before mine. I am glad I did that for others, but it is now time for me to see who and what I can become.

Besides, if our professor can accomplish all he has in his first twenty-three years, I can get control of my life at this stage because I have learned so much in the many years I have lived. With all of you helping me, I have already won and so have all of you by being brave enough to leave your comfort zone and now let each one of us support each other in becoming better speakers, presenters of information, and better people in the next eighteen weeks than we were before tonight," she said, looking at all of us who suddenly became her strongest supporters.

The class immediately began applauding so she knew instantly just how much those words inspired them and made the class feel capable of overcoming the fears each one had about public speaking. She had touched the hearts of those who had been given the opportunity to hear her speech. Not only was there applause, but almost instantly, the entire class was giving Caudie Brown a standing ovation.

When the students who were standing in front of me, because I was at the back of the classroom, sat down, I saw a smile, tears of joy, and a humbleness of a master teacher standing before those willing to listen and able to learn because she was finally able to shed the past fears that had made her feel inferior and now allowed her to face her future!

For the next seven speeches that were required in the course, Caudie taught us what it was like to have a new self-confidence, what one needed to do to be prepared in both research and rehearsal of presentation, and to have great topic choices.

I loved that at least once in each of her speeches, she had a saying that I made a mantra for my life from that class forward when she would say, "Truth be told" to let us know how important it is to always tell the truth but house it in a way that allows other people to ponder what they are hearing and consider it to become their new truth.

She was so good that I found myself demanding more from her than the others because she wanted to become so effective, and I wanted her to learn as much as possible. My critiques of her work may have appeared harsher than some of the other students, but it was done because she was so superior, and I could talk about the very picky things instead of the general concepts that most beginning public speakers displayed.

I tried to get Caudie to join the speech team several times during the semester. She always had an excuse of being too old, too busy, or that her husband would not let her. I knew it was not the last reason or she would not have been taking my class. She found in our class an opportunity to give herself just what she wanted; self-confidence, self-assurance, and the strength to begin to do things for herself without asking permission from others. Those things were all she was able to accept at that moment in time.

The last class was full of celebration and reflection. That class will always be one of my favorite classes. It may have taken place because it was my first semester of teaching college courses. It may have been because of my age and the outstanding older students who accepted me from the beginning and did not question my expertise. It may have been because the rural areas of America have little resources to turn to when wanting to get a higher education. I will never know why for sure; but what I do know is that class proved to me I was where I needed to be at that time in my life.

At the end of class, many of the students lingered in the classroom. I had collected my things and was about to exit when I was asked if I wanted to go with some of them to have a drink to celebrate the collective growth that had been accomplished. I had heard one student say,

"Do you think he would like to go with us?"

"We do think he is old enough, don't we?" asked another student. Claudie did as only she could do, and asked me,

"We are going to have a drink to celebrate what you taught us and hopefully what we taught you.

Would you like to come?"

"Of course." I went with them!

Once we got to the bar, one by one, the students ordered their drinks. Only Caudie and I were left. The waitress looked at her. She looked at me. I spoke:

"She will have a Pink Lady and I will have a Screwdriver." Suddenly one by one the following things were said.

"Ok, now what just happened?"

"How do you know what she drinks?"

"Have the two of you come here prior to tonight?"

"Excuse you Mr. Reel, I thought you might want an older person. Excuse me, Miss Caudie!"

"Stop! Now that the class is over, I will share, Caudie Brown, is my older sister." I announced.

"So, that is what they are calling it now?"

"You treated her much harder than you treated the rest of us."

"Sometimes you were so critical with her, I thought you disliked her because she was so good!"

I felt it was time to talk again. I picked up my

glass that had just arrived and proposed a toast.

"Let's toast the best class I have ever taught and to how each of you exceeded your own expectations!" I called out because the bar was now louder than when we arrived. Caudie never competed in speech. She did take some art classes. When her husband died, she decided to return to Oklahoma where she had been born. She made her own decisions for the rest of her life doing as she wanted. She taught me to take responsibility for my own actions. She taught me to live responsibly and to allow myself to make an error, but then learn from it and correct the situation. "Truth be told," she was a tremendous influence on my life.

CHAPTER FOUR:
BAKERSFIELD COLLEGE

ReAnne Rioski

My mother taught me early in life to never tell anyone that you will never do a certain thing. I thought I would never date someone to keep them from judging one of my debate teams, but as it happened that is exactly what I did. We had attended five tournaments and my debate team was getting noticed by the coaching staff of prestigious schools like USC, Redlands, Pepperdine, UCLA, Cal Poly, and even Georgetown.

When we traveled to a tournament, coaches from those very highly sought after colleges, would make it a point to ask if either of my two debaters had committed to a school after community college. It helped immensely, the two of them were being recognized consistently as one of the top four speakers in each tournament. In fact, they were either winning or taking second place in all but one tournament. They were quickly gaining notoriety as a team to beat if you were lucky, and a team you did not want to face in the last few preliminary rounds or any of the elimination rounds. You would be eliminated!

One judge, ReAnne Rioski, did not like them for some reason. She found a way to vote against them every time she judged them. At first, I thought the guys were just being paranoid about her. We ran a tabulation at each of the contests, and 95% of the rounds they lost, she was the judge.

My team and her team thought it would be cute if the two of us started dating. Her top team, two girls, would borrow evidence and analysis from my team, and they would share information regarding what cases other teams were arguing when those other teams were on the affirmative side of the topic.

I could not get out of my head what the boys had told me about trying to date her so she would not judge them and vote against them every single time she judged them. She always said just enough to vote the way she chose, but when she was with at least two other judges, it was always two votes for us, and one vote against us. It was a tournament at UCLA when I seized on the opportunity to ask her out. I was at the campus bookstore when I saw her just ahead of me in line to purchase some debate supplies. I was there to purchase a shirt, running trunks, and a sweatshirt with the UCLA logo. I was making a clothing collection to document the places where my team had competed. I walked behind her.

"Good afternoon. I snuck away thinking most other coaches and judges might be judging instead of shopping at this hour. However, it is not only a pleasure to meet you, but also the first of what I hope will be an everyday blessing for me to see you inside and outside of the forensics world." I said, smiling as convincingly as possible.

"Well, imagine you away from the posting signs and team gathering areas. What will that incredible team of yours do without you when they get out of the round and don't receive coaching from you regarding their next round?" she asked in a matter-of-fact tone and loudness.

"I think they would be pleased because for some reason, they think you don't like them and always vote against them," I said trying to come off with humor but meaning every word I said. I wanted her to know I wanted to get to the bottom of why she consistently gave us a loss.

"I don't think I am the only judge that votes against your team," ReAnne said smiling. I could tell why she was liked by many of the male judges. She was dressed in a higher quality of clothing than most of the other women judges; her hair was colored with highlights that complimented the dark blonde, and lighter blonde shades that was bottle generated, and the highlights of three different other blonde colors. She looked amazing as a blonde!

"You are one judge who rarely, if ever, votes for

them. I just want to know what it is they would have to do to win your vote in any round?" I asked, feeling I had nothing to lose, because she was not voting for them in any round of competition.

"Is this judging shame or intimidation?" she asked, smiling a beautiful smile. I could tell her parents had spent thousands of dollars on that smile, or she had the most perfect human genetic system going in the entire world.

"I don't think anyone from Bakersfield could shame or intimate anyone like yourself. You are too educated for anyone to think you did not vote your conscience.

"I always vote the way I feel will teach the debaters the most. Sometimes, a loss makes them want to do better and they are stronger because of what I say," she said confidently.

"I am not saying you were wrong. We just want to know what it is that you are looking for in the round as to reasoning, evidence, or analysis that they can add to help them be clearer and stronger," I responded as quickly as possible.

"The arguments presented by both in the first speeches make absolute sense and are creative and make me want to vote for them. Something seems to change as the debate progresses. During the rebuttal time, I feel they choose the wrong arguments to respond to and keep alive in the debate." she said holding firm and appearing convinced of her position.

"Well, I will sit down with them and find out which arguments they are stressing during the rebuttals, and reexamine why they are dropping the other arguments," I said smiling and wanting to find a way to ask her out.

"Perhaps I could go over some of my old debate notes concerning those debate rounds with you sometime," she said taking her credit card from a Gucci purse. She was pretty and bright.

"I would love to do that, but almost all of my time at these tournaments is occupied by my meeting all the times I have free with them," I said explaining why it would not be at a tournament.

"There is time outside of the debate world, you know. We should not be tied down to our jobs *ALL* of the time. I love to do *ALL* the things every other girl likes," she said. She winked at me when she finished.

"What would be something you would love to do sometime in the near future?" I asked, thinking it might be a stroll to the beach.

"There is a new singer coming to the Universal Outdoor Stadium I would love to see!" she said while smiling as only she could.

"What is the performers name?" I asked. I had to ask because I did not have time to listen to the radio and knew I would not know the person.

"Elton John," she said.

"Is he American?" I asked.

"No, he is part of the 'British Invasion' who have arrived and are taking over," she said smiling and giggling like she had maneuvered me to get to where she wanted to go. She quickly made a tremendous impact on my life as both a forensics coach and as a person. She began driving to

Bakersfield two or three times a week, and on the rare weekends we did not have tournaments, I would go south to be close to her.

It was not long before we were known as a couple and our physical contact in public did not allow her to judge my debate team. By the end of the first year, we were dating no other persons. She was contemplating leaving the teaching field and going to a top-level management position for one of the largest and most prestigious companies in Los Angeles, the *Bloomingdale Company*. It was a very important decision because it more than doubled her teaching salary.

Her parents knew we were serious, and wanted

to have a meeting with both of us to discuss how and what we would need to do to ensure the financial stability of what they called a "Merged Enterprise." They felt ReAnne would be marrying down in social status if she married me and felt their daughter should consider the consequences of such a decision. Teachers, professors, and any school employee in administration did not make near the salary I was offered to come into the family and help construct the legacy that already was identified by the family. It did not include ReAnne staying in education or with the *Bloomingdale Company* after the age of thirty.

It was a very hard choice for me to make. I so loved and had devoted my entire being from the age of eighteen to be the best I could be in my profession. I could not allow my decision to be made over money. I knew I could make a living that was comfortable and if I found the right person who wanted to share it with me, we could be content. She gave into the demands of her parents. ReAnne and her family taught me that some families are about enriching a legacy through financial gain at the cost of love.

She taught me that love cannot be bought but rather nourished into something that two people can do sharing the same vision without interference from others.

CHAPTER FIVE: BAKERSFIELD COLLEGE

Daniel Turner

A t the end of the sixth week of classes, I needed to evaluate each student to see if they were doing below average (grade less than "C") work so I could send out official notification to alert them of their status in the class. I only had four students who were functioning below the 70% level in all the courses I was teaching.

Daniel Turner was a gifted speaker. He had a great personality and it shined when he spoke. His introduction speech was very moving and showed his drive to make something of himself and to leave the valley through the opportunity of going to college, playing football, and hopefully having an NFL career. I had been so busy; I had not paid attention to the fact he had missed several classes the last two weeks including a major test.

Daniel was a running back and had asked me to attend one of our home games. When I calculated his score, it was 61 percent. I quickly completed the paperwork to notify the college administration, the athletic director, and the student.

I called the phone number that was listed on the class enrollment paperwork. There was no answer. I sent a note to the athletic director asking for a meeting so we could work on the solution together.

The next morning as I arrived for my office hour, a tall man wearing a Bakersfield College jacket was waiting at my door.

"Good morning," he said. He reached his hand out to shake mine.

"Good morning," I said. I put my office key in the lock, opened the door, and then walked behind my desk and sat down.

"I am Randal Killingsbee, an assistant director of athletics. I got your notice regarding Daniel Turner. You do know he is ranked the number one running back in our league this season, don't you?" he asked, taking a seat directly in front of me.

"I did not know that. He did tell us during his introduction speech he was a member of what he thought would be a team that had a chance to win the league title. That makes this meeting even more important because we need to find a way to ensure he passes this class with at least a "C" grade," I said, making the case, I wanted to work to find a solution. Before I could continue, he interrupted.

"You need to get on board with our athletic protocol at this college of passing our athletes. It is no accident you have five of our starters in your classes. We are testing the waters with you to see if you understand your duty to your new employer. He must be at the "C" level. It is easy to change. I have a grade change form with me. You can use error, mistake, or incompetence as your justification. You must come up with a reason!" he demanded. He wanted me to be offended and allow anger or rage to take over. He wanted me to be upset and become unmanageable. Instead, I positioned myself to be in control of the situation.

"I know of a better solution. Why not help our Daniel earn a passing grade? We still have half of a semester left to help him. He did not take the last test and that reduced his entire grade for the course. I am willing to allow him to come to my office today or tomorrow and to take it and I will enter that score into the total points earned, which should be enough to get him back where he needs to be so he will be eligible to play," I said pushing back so he knew he was not going to bully me.

"This is the very difficult time of the season when we are calling special practices, extra weight training sessions, and running drills,... you get the drift...so, sometimes our schedule interferes with their classes. These athletes need to take a step back away from their classes that might interfere with what might be their only hope at getting out of this place they currently call home," he said raising his voice.

"I don't think this conversation is going in the direction I thought it would concerning the true welfare of our mutual students (not just an athlete, but most importantly, a STUDENT!

The college states in its mission statement their EDUCATION (not sports) is the core value of what this college stands for. You will not intimidate nor require, nor demand I provide grades that are not earned by any student. Again, let me make myself clear as possible so you can relay my position to any person above your pay grade who sent you here to do their work! I *will not* be intimidated! My students will not be bought! You are no longer allowed to be in my office. I am going to only ask this question once, and if I don't get the answer and the result I want, I will be calling security and have you escorted from this room. Will you leave now?" I asked in a very slow, deliberate, and forceful voice.

"I will leave, but unless you choose to cooperate with us, your stay at this college won't be long. We are part of the college that will oversee your tenure process here. That process takes three years to complete. Anywhere along the way, you may be dismissed without cause. You don't want to have your colleagues across the state find out you could not even last one year, do you?

We have many people who support our efforts throughout this college ranging from peers, lowerlevel administrators, and up the ladder as far as it is needed. You just won't know who your friend or foe is until it is too late!" he said standing and walking toward the door.

"I will not fall for such threats. If I must work under those conditions, I will choose to leave, and it will be on my own terms, and I will do all I can to see this type of intimidation behavior does not continue. Your name will be the first I call out. I can get a job almost anywhere when I apply. I doubt you can say that! If things come out about what you are doing to our students, you may be the one who is out of a job!" I called out so he could hear my words as he exited.

Within an hour, I had a call from a secretary from the athletics department.

"Mr. Reel, it appears some type of mistake or misunderstanding has taken place between you and one of our assistant coaches. Is there a time when you might come by and talk directly with another one of assistant athletic directors?" she asked.

"I don't think a misunderstanding took place. I won't be talking to any other assistant. If Director Adams would like to discuss this issue, he can make an appointment with me to see me in my office," I said, pausing to hear what she would say next.

"I am sure I can arrange for you to see Director Adams, but it will have to be here in his office," she said.

"I teach interpersonal communication and I don't plan to go to where Mr. Adams feels he has additional power. If he wants to talk with me, you can make an appointment for him during my office hours and in my office. They are posted on my door. I have a class to go to now where students will show up to earn their education!" I said deliberately hanging the phone down gently so she would know I was not slamming it down because I lost control and anger was not an issue. I needed not only to teach interpersonal skills, but to live by what is taught. Learning is always a two-sided adventure.

When I returned to my office after class, I found a message that informed me Mr. Adams would be meeting me the next day during my office hours. She informed me the meeting would be at my office and asked me to clear my schedule for at least thirty minutes. I knew then I would have to stand firm on the values needed to be honored so that higher education really did mean something.

Mr. Adams arrived at my office right on time. I deliberately had arrived early and had the door closed so he would have to notify me when he arrived. He knocked three times loudly.

"The door is unlocked, please come in," I said while staying seated at my desk. I was going to make him come to me on my terms. He opened the door and entered my office. I had not met him before. He was tall, had gray hair, a beard, and was dressed in a suit. He did not offer to shake my hand. He stood prepared to talk to and not with me.

"Mr. Reel, I am here to make the problem go...:" I interrupted him,

"Please have a seat so we can have this conversation and hopefully arrive at an acceptable way out for both of us." I spoke. Again, I motioned for him to take a seat in the chair I had arranged off center to give him less power. I was sure he wanted to stand so he would exhibit power, but I was not going to allow this to happen.

"I am OK standing if you don't mind," he said preparing to continue his speech.

"It is not OK; we are both adults and I want to discuss this with you person to person. If you insist on standing, then I will stand and we can go outside so we are in equal proximity," I responded. He sat down.

"That is fine. Exactly why are you here? I hope it is to find out how Daniel can pass my class legitimately," I declared.

"Our athletes are very important to this college. Football alone brings 75% of the nonstate revenue and is the most funds generated by the college. Everyone knows that if you want or need money it must come through the athletic department.

We need to find colleagues who will help ensure that we allow those students who have certain kinds of obstacles in their lives that hinder their superior efforts for us on the athletic field not be a problem while they are here. We look after their wellbeing by providing food, medicines, places to live if needed, and training. We have the best trainers and coaches we can find. They need to put all their efforts in the arena that fits them better than anything else." he told me as a great storyteller would.

"But what about why they are here? Where does their education take place in your world?" I asked.

"Their world is sports," he said.

"No, that is your world. They are supposed to manage in both. I am glad we have such high standards that bring talented people to assist them in that one part of their education. However, it is only one part." I started moving slightly to him to demonstrate a change from the equal power I had been allowing.

"Not all these kids are smart enough to get through all the classes needed to earn a degree. They are here only to do sports. Hell, ninety percent don't complete an associate degree. We are using them as ambassadors from us to our community. Our stadium is very important to the community. We are ranked as one of the finest track and field arenas in all of California. We need athletes like Daniel to bring that attention to our program and to support our budget." Mr. Adams had declared sports to be the only area that mattered, and academics were not really a part of the life of the athletes.

"If Daniel comes back to class and gives his speeches and takes his tests he can pass. I will not pass him because he is your athlete; he is my student," I declared as I stood up overshadowing him.

"Mr. Reel you are making the worst decision of your young life. My connections will be subtle at first but will have you out of this college soon!" he said, standing and walking to the door.

"You may be older than me, but you are not wiser or better. Threats and corrupted power will never win in the end!" I said in a louder voice than he had used.

Daniel came back to class the next day. He participated in class discussions and critiques of fellow students. When the class was over and as the students walked out, I said,

"Daniel, thanks for being in class today. Can we find time for you to make up that missed test?" I said, as I moved toward him.

"Mr. Reel, I appreciate that you want me to learn something in your class. My other teachers have all said just come when I can fit it into my schedule; but all I must do is show up. You expect me to prepare, and I like the fact that you think I can, but Coach has enrolled me in another speech class starting tomorrow. I just wanted to come by today to say thanks for seeing more in me than sports," he said looking down. We were now standing next to each other. We were the only two in the room.

"Look, you are capable. You can do the work!

Don't let anyone use you for their gain. What do you think you're going to get out of switching classes?" I asked, wanting to know his wants and desires.

"I want to get the hell out of here and make a life for me that will show people I am important," he shared with tears developing.

"You are important. You can do the work required by any course this college has to offer. You are much more than just an athlete. I know you can find the time to do both if you want. I can even help you in your other classes if you just come by and see me during my office hours. I will find the time outside of them if I need to." I pleaded. He finally looked up and our eyes met.

"I am really good at football. Some say if I leave and go to UCLA and start for them, I have a great chance to make the pros! All my worries will be over, and I can get my parents a nice house and life will be good," he said moving forward and closer to me. I could tell this was one of the first times he felt close enough to an educator to share his feelings unmasked and hoped he would not regret sharing his feelings. He wanted some type of validation. I wanted to be part of that moment. He wanted it too.

"If you are that good, and as articulate as you are, go to all your classes and learn all the other information you will need to take all the worries away. Don't take the easy way, take the way that will give you more opportunities. What happens if you get hurt or you don't make it to the pros? Use your education as a backup for sports. I will be your most ardent supporter," I said, now crying myself.

"Coach says the profs we are assigned will be OK once class starts if we just stop coming. We can get a passing grade," he said trying to justify the propaganda he had been given.

"That means you are going to get lower grades than if you did the work and came to class. You can earn either an "A" or "B" in my class if you take your missing test and you do well in your last two presentations." I said, as calmly as possible.

"Thanks for believing in me, but I plan to only be at UCLA for one year and be an NFL running back by the time I am twenty-one years old. I will use college as my fallback if needed," Daniel said as he turned and walked out of my office. I never saw him again. No one sent me any official information about a transfer, so at the end of the semester I gave him a letter grade of "F" for my course.

Daniel did make it to the pros for a few years. I heard from the Rally Club on campus how successful he was for a short time playing in the NFL.

Unfortunately, he suffered a serious injury, and to the best of my knowledge, he never became the star he had wanted to be for very long. He would have benefited from having something to fall back on after his professional career. Daniel taught me to try harder to convince vulnerable young students caught up in the glamour of potential wealth of professional sports to insist on a back-up plan. Professional athletic statistics claim that just 1.6 percent of college football players will become an NFL player. So, the other 98.4 percent of players in college will not have their dream realized. These statistics prove one should establish a solid back-up plan, which often is the course of action that is needed after the allure of fame has not been realized. Daniel taught me that back-up plans do provide useful alternatives.

CHAPTER SIX:
BAKERSFIELD COLLEGE

Melody Notes

I needed some women on our speech team. I found the answer to my problem in my public speaking class. As luck would have it, my first assignment in public speaking was to not only inform us about something, but to talk about something not commonly known. Melody, who was beautiful, quiet, and able to remember my lectures perfectly. She would ask questions that made it fun for me to teach because I had to be more than just prepared for each class. Her speech was on *The History of the California Car Show Models.* Her visual aids consisted of blownup pictures showing how the female calendar car models had changed over the decades. It was pointed to showcase the attire that had changed the look of modeling in what was deemed appropriate clothing. I had given her speech presentation grade a "98" out of "100," She earned "100" out of "100" for her visual aids. Her last visual aid was a picture of her accepting the *"Miss California Car Shows Model"* award. After class, I asked her to come by my office as soon as possible. She arrived the next day halfway through the hour. My door was open.

"Mr. Reel, you asked me to stop by. Here I am," she said. She was so stunning it almost took my breath away.

"Yes, thanks for stopping by for a quick chat. I was so impressed with your speech; I thought you should share it with others. I coach the speech team and I think your speech could be very competitive," I said standing and moving toward her.

"That is very kind, but I work weekends at

Denny's and don't think I can ask for the time off; and besides, that is the best time to make tips," she said walking into my office. She sat down and shared the real reason she did not want to do forensics.

"I love speaking in public, but I have this fear I will lose. I can't see myself doing as well as others. It took me three attempts to be *Miss California Car Shows Model.*

"Everyone experiences some type of fear. Public Speaking is the second most fear people experience other than death, according to behavioral magazines that monitor such statistics. While there are five to six other contestants speaking in a competition round, you are competing only against yourself to see how effective your speech is at that given minute with that judge. You are ready to go with that speech." I said, trying not to let her get away.

"But what about work?" she asked.

"I am sure they will understand if I write a letter on school letterhead that informs them there are fieldtrips, and part of your class will be graded on attendance and interaction with other students." I said, providing an excuse she could use for work.

"How many weekends would I miss?" she asked.

"Five or six weekends between now and the end of April," I said trying to get as much distance between what might seem too many.

"Really?" she asked. I could tell she was considering her options.

"About once a month is all that will be required. I bet you will be one of the most successful speakers we have on the team. I would even suggest you try persuasive speaking as a second event!" I spoke.

Melody did become much more than *Ms.*

California Car Shows. She used her competitive speech as a steppingstone to the next few levels that helped her become an intern, an assistant, and eventually she entered law school and ultimately became a successful attorney. She took the risk of overcoming something she feared, and it changed her life for the better. Melody taught me to see life as progressing through life by taking baby steps that are safe and if necessary, allows one to adjust in small increments so you have time to learn from each experience.

CHAPTER SEVEN: BAKERSFIELD COLLEGE

Wendy Morrison and Tim Sneed

My Wasco evening class was especially interesting because so many of the students were older. None of them had time or energy to consider participating in my forensics team at the college. Yet, one of the three younger students in the class gave me some hope. Wendy approached me after class one evening. I had finished collecting my materials when I saw she was waiting at the door.

"Wendy, did you forget something? May I assist with anything? Have you lost something?" I asked her as I started to move toward the door to leave the classroom.

"Yes, I have an idea how I can help you and your forensics team. It is not me, but a friend of mine is at the main campus, and he would be great!" she declared.

"I certainly would entertain meeting with him on campus if you let him know that all he would need to do is drop by my office," I suggested.

"I will need to bring him with me, and he won't know exactly why he is accompanying me. I may have told him I wanted to join but did not have the courage to come and talk to you without him," she confessed even though I was not a priest.

"We may be able to use both of you. You could certainly participate in the program from what I have seen in this class. What is your friend's name, and what makes him a worthy candidate?" I inquired.

"His name is Tim, and he has won all kinds of speaking tournaments. He got all the way to the state finals in the *Kiwanis Club* competitions. His specialty is persuasive speaking. He is very dramatic and knows many statistics," she said, smiling as though she had just revealed a great secret.

"I don't like deception. Why don't you tell him you want both of you to talk with me about forensics?" I countered.

"After four years of very close friendship, I know what will make him happy. I can never be as good as he will be, but if it takes me to try to get him to do this, I will give it a try." she said demonstrating her care and understanding of her friend. She made one last point before she left for the evening.

"You won't be sorry for allowing him to participate on your team. He will rise to the top, and I will come along for the ride. Don't expect too much from me," she said smiling and turning to go out the door.

"I will expect a lot from both of you. That is all anyone can expect and if that is done, we all will be happy and blessed!" I said as the door was about to close.

Wendy and Tim always met together with me. I never practiced with them together, but one would be scheduled for rehearsal and then the other. One would wait or go to the library while the other person rehearsed. This couple was quite the talk of the forensics team.

She was only four years older than Tim but looked about ten years older. He appeared to be two or three years younger than his real age. Most people thought Tim to be about sixteen and Wendy about twenty-four. At that phase of life, the age difference was somewhat a question for some. The younger team members seemed more alarmed than the older more mature members. Today I can't think of anyone who would consider this age grouping an issue.

True to what Wendy said concerning Tim, he was even better than she had predicted. The creativity, the word choice, the presentation, and his spot-on delivery could be better mastered by only a few. His topic was how college educated parents gave their children an unfair advantage over others. His statistics indicated the divide widened the more educated the parents and those with none or little education. Tim had an interesting take on this topic. His father was highly educated, while his mother was not. Both parents, after divorcing, decided to raise him to the best of their own abilities. Tim's mother was at a distinct disadvantage financially because she never continued her education, climbed up the employment ladder, or was ever going to be a homeowner. Tim's father was very wealthy and able to provide tutors, educational camps, and many trips abroad for his son. He wanted him to experience the world as a teaching tool.

As I coached him, I relied on the memory of how Ginger Vogler, my coach at San Joaquin Delta College, had acted when I first started my public speaking career. Tim wanted to make his mother proud and show her she had brought up a son that could compete against those from a higher social economic group and be a winner. Ginger taught me the power of establishing eye contact with the audience.

He began winning tournaments and was quite popular among the individual events contestants. As his popularity increased, so did his self-confidence. He began looking at people directly establishing direct eye contact. He asked questions of others about their family, major, and truly wanted to know things that mattered about people whom he had met.

By the end of the year, Tim had branched out into the Lincoln-Douglas debate category. He was participating in three events: persuasive speaking, informative speaking, and now a form of debate.

Lincoln-Douglas is a competition debate with only one person on each side. His emotion and statistics were a true asset for this event. The problem we had was trying to find people that were willing to debate in this division. My top debate team would occasionally split-up and practice with him, but the style, format, and delivery aspects were completely different.

Tim and Wendy remained friends during the college years. Wendy became an attorney, and Tim taught school, then he also became an attorney. They started a practice together, but eventually separated their legal practice and dissolved their marriage. This couple taught me two people from any socioeconomic group can become best friends, then be involved romantically, and eventually work together professionally. They also taught me that when working full-time with your romantic partner as well as your business partner, it places additional stress and responsibility on the relationship; and unless both parties are willing to spend additional time working on the personal relationship, it seems to dissolve. Keeping a personal relationship with another person takes time, effort, and energy.

CHAPTER EIGHT: BAKERSFIELD COLLEGE

Led Rapkin

We had secured an old supply closet at the end of one of the classroom buildings for our practice room. It was not very large, and we had only a table, four chairs where the debaters would sit, and a student chair/desk where I would sit while listening to the practice sessions. The debaters would put their evidence on the tables, their notepads for keeping track of what was said, and that was all that could be accommodated.

The room was not very well insulated for heat or noise. We kept the door open most of the time so anyone near could see when it was occupied. The slogan for our team was; *if the door was open, learning was taking place.* One day we were in the middle of a practice debate between myself and Tim when the door opened and both he and I were surprised by the person we met. We had never been disturbed when we were in the practice room. It was a safe haven for trying new arguments and seeking help.

"What the hell is all of this noise coming from this room?" he asked. I did not recognize him but knew he was not a faculty member, custodial staff, or administrator.

"We are practicing debate," I responded. I now looked at him more closely. He had long hair, wore a camouflage coat like those worn in Viet Nam, had a backpack, and was smoking.

"Does it have to be so loud? I am a man of peaceful existence and just walking past this room was disturbing to me and my tranquility. I am trying to find Mr. Reel, because my counselor told me he might benefit from my knowledge, vocabulary, and wanting to find something to do with my time." he said, waiting to see if we could help.

"This room echoes, and we try to be less loud when possible. I am Mr. Reel. I am the speech coach.

Are you considering doing some public speaking?" I asked pausing our debate.

"I have spent the last four years of my life reading everything I could. I have read humorous books, the ancients, novels, comic books, trivia books, specialty books, well, as I said, all I could. I read all the time. Books have become my best friends. I like them better than people. People judge me. Books don't. When I didn't know the definition of a word, I looked it up; when I didn't know how to say a word, I found out how to pronounce the word. Tell me what you're discussing and see if I can contribute?" he asked, putting his cigarette out in a can he took from his backpack.

"You may be the person we are looking for at this minute, but we don't even know your name," I said hoping that he would provide it.

"Led Rapkin at your service," he quickly responded standing at attention as he called out his name.

"Well, what we need desperately is another Lincoln-Douglas debater. Tim is our only one currently, and it is hard to have practice debates with just one person. Have you thought about debating?" I asked, hoping this new walking encyclopedia of knowledge standing a few feet from me would want to join us as badly as I needed him. I wondered what it would take to get him to become a team member.

"I am tired of visiting with my professors after each class, and "Truth be told," most of them are pretty damn boring. They don't even always meet during their promised office hours. So, you gents are in luck because I think it is time, I learn something new," he said putting his backpack down and waiting for instructions.

I was intrigued by him saying what Caudie Brown had said so many times. I felt it must have been a sign from either God or the universe.

"You will have to enroll in the class and be accountable   for attendance,   participation,   and attending at least four tournaments per semester," I barked out doing my best imitation of a drill sergeant.

"One additional class will neither break nor get in the way of my reasons for attending a junior college prior to me transferring to a major university. I am all about minimalism and I am saving as much of my money as I can. Besides, Uncle Sam is shouldering all of my tuition, books, and even giving me a stipend in addition for the time I spent keeping you boys free," he said with great pride.

"When do you think, you might want to start?" I asked, hoping it would be soon. We needed someone to compliment Tim. I already knew they could learn from each other.

"How about right now? I have about an hour. Can I learn how to do this during my free time today?" he asked smiling, while reaching into his pocket taking out a rubber band and taking both hands and putting his long hair behind the back of his neck.

"Take a seat. You need a legal-size pad to take notes, two different colored pens to keep track of what you want to say and what your opponents say," I instructed him as though he would know what my command meant.

"Hold on a minute. I don't usually take notes, I just free style when I talk. I can remember most of what was said and take my time when responding to my points of view," Led said.

"You are going to be under strict time requirements and during the main speeches you have slightly more time than the rebuttals," I instructed in my official professorial voice.

"Let's just try me out without all your formal stuff. I am an individual and don't want to adhere to preconceived notions or requirements. I think I will be refreshing for people who have been caged up with all this formality," Led predicted, expressing who he really was in that moment and sharing how he approached life.

"The topic this year is, 'Resolved: That the United States should significantly change the method of selecting presidential and vice-presidential candidates.' This is the formal topic we must debate for competition this year."

"I don't need much research on that topic. For God's sake, scholars have for a long time warned against the electoral college method compared to having a straight popular vote. That way, each person who does vote, makes that vote matter instead of electing people you don't even know get to vote. Is that something that might be considered?" Led debated convincingly and ended it with a question.

"We need to help you with first making a statement of what point you are making or clarifying, but yes that sounds like you might have a career in Lincoln-Douglas Debate." I spoke in amazement at what I had just heard. Led did it his way and wound up going to the final round at the next tournament. By the time we got to the State Finals, he was one of the most feared debaters. By nationals, he had his own groupies following him. He always did it his way! It paid off and he returned home as a national champion.

Led taught me never to judge any student by the first impression they make. Not one single student stayed exactly as when I met them the first time and I assessed my first impression. I had not gone to Viet Nam, and he taught me to stop judging those who returned as less than those who had stayed home. My twin served in the military but did not have to go to Viet Nam. I tried to enlist, but because I had Rheumatic Fever as a child, the military would not accept me. All our service persons should be honored for their service and dedication. I truly believe that Led taught me to respect and fight for the rights of those who chose to do what I was unable to do; serve our country.

CHAPTER NINE: BAKERSFIELD COLLEGE

Atlanta Heartbreak

I felt so proud of the team as we headed to Atlantic in the spring of my second year for the National Phi Rho Pi Speech Final Tournament. The "Survivors" as I called them had come together and we had a chance to be one of the top teams at the tournament. Todd had taken the lead in coordinating the various students, their wants, needs, and rallied them not only to want what was best for their own selfish reasons, but also to see what it would be like to be a part of something bigger by contributing to a team effort to set our school apart from so many others. Todd had taken on participating in Oral Interpretation of Literature, but also had branched out into After Dinner Speaking.

Terry and DeWayne had come from novice to open division in debate. In fact, they were ranked among the top four teams attending the tournament.

The two of them had sacrificed much time and effort, to rehearse, research, and practice against anyone that would debate them, including me!

Terry had started competing in Impromptu Speaking and DeWayne was participating in Extemporaneous Speaking. The team members felt both would automatically be in the final round in these events. Melody not only had captivated the male judges with her informative speech on the *History of Car Show Models*, most women contestants and judges gave her outstanding remarks for informing about a topic that was very original and had never been heard about in competition before her speech. She was also competitive in Persuasive Speaking.

Wendy and Tim had blossomed into competitive speakers in both Informative and Persuasive Speaking. Tim was also competitive in Lincoln-Douglas Debate. Led was the person to beat in Lincoln-Douglas Debate. Todd, Melody, Wendy, and Tim came together in the Reader's Theatre competition with a show entitled, *"The Wonderful World of Dr. Seuss."* The team had come a long way that first year. It is very hard for a team to earn a reputation, but ours did it.

Most teams take at least five years to earn respect from other coaches, a reputation among competitors, and to create an anticipation of excellence in the minds of the judges at the college level. Teams which have such recognition have an advantage when a student from that college enters a competition room because it is taken for granted that the speaker will be excellent and competitively vying for the top ranking. At first, my students would lose to a team or individual that had a better reputation. Early during the first semester, whether it be debate or individual events, my students would not be ranked as they should have been because they were not known.

They received comments like, "You are truly superior, and it was a difficult decision on my part, but I felt while you are very close to success, a second place from me should send a message that you are certainly on the right track." Such a reputation is also seen at local high schools within the immediate vicinity of where the college is located. My students started going out to the local high school competitions and acting as judges. They began recruiting future students. Students want to come and join a team that is known to be caring and successful. By the end of the first year, we had several students wanting to come and join our team from the immediate high school community.

DeWayne had personally given the most because of his homelife (or lack of) it. Terry, DeWayne, and I had driven at least ten times to do specific case research at UCLA, USC, and Stanford because they were among the top five college libraries in California. Terry always had money for food provided by his parents, while DeWayne had none.

Before each trip started, I would hand DeWayne a twenty-dollar bill when greeting him. I also made sure he had proper clothes to match the new suits, had haircuts when needed, and even provided him with new frames for his glasses when he broke them and taped them instead of asking for new ones. He had become the younger brother I wanted to succeed in life because I knew if anyone could do it, he could. The boys were doing their full-time job of being great students and superior debaters.

Between teaching, meeting my office hours, rehearsing with all the individual events people, debating practices, writing a readers' theatre script, rehearsing, and preparing it for competition, there was little time for my personal life. ReAnne was very understanding and accommodating to my hectic schedule. We had become serious; because we both loved speech and she quickly helped coach some of my students as well as her own. She would even listen to Terry and DeWayne when I needed them not to forget how to adapt to what we called a "lay judge" or an individual events coach who wanted communication skills to outweigh a great amount of evidence and did not appreciate the direction that speed debate was moving. She helped them to remember to be persuasive. Her willingness to critique them made them realize the most important task for competitors and that was to adapt to the judge. They started asking judges before the round started what type of debate style they preferred. She had worked her magic!

It was my first-time visiting Atlanta. As I look back on that trip, it wasn't really a visit to Atlanta. We landed at the airport, a bus took us to the hotel where not only did we stay, but the tournament was held on site. The competition started early each morning and would finish early in the evening. We had a team meeting each morning one hour before the competition started so I could meet with the entire team at one time.

We used this time to address any issues that needed attention, reaffirm the morning competition events, allow the students to perform the speech they would be giving first a complete run through, and let them know how proud I was they were representing our college, me, and most importantly, themselves. At one of our team meetings, DeWayne was not engaged. He was constantly looking down and not being a team leader. He was not smiling and was not contributing. When I dismissed the group, I motioned to him:

"DeWayne, may I see you for just a minute?" I asked. He started walking in the opposite direction from where I was standing.

"DeWayne, I need you for just a minute," I said a bit louder. I also moved toward him. He saw me but kept walking. I walked faster and arrived beside him and Terry.

"DeWayne, what is the matter? Let's talk about what is up?"

"Nothing Coach," he said as he continued looking down but had stopped walking.

"I don't think that is true. You are not your usual self. You can tell me." I said hoping he would share.

"I said nothing is the matter. Let it go," he said, but I could hear the cracking of his voice that one gets right before crying starts.

"We have come too far, and I care too much for you not to be able to tell me anything." I said, now facing him directly placing my hands on his shoulders.

"This tournament is going to be over tomorrow and everyone except me will go home to their families. I don't have one," he blurted out now trying to keep from crying so all would see.

"You have a family. We are your family!" I said, giving him a hug. It was coming directly from my heart to someone who was so deserving to have a real family.

"It's not the same!" he said almost under his breath.

"When we get back, I will help you find a place of your own," I said believing with the people I knew DeWayne could not only get financial assistance, but also some well-deserved counseling that would help him with anger issues that he sometimes displayed. He would get angry and usually storm off for a few minutes and then return as though nothing had happened.

"I have found my own place," he said turning to walk to his round of extemporaneous speaking.

"That is great news. I will help you with decorating it when we get back. We want a special place for all the trophies you are going to win,"

I yelled as he walked away. He turned around, smiled, and I felt we had weathered another storm.

When the tournament got to the fourth round

of debate, Terry and DeWayne were hitting a team that had won their state tournament. The same thing happened round five. In round six, we hit a team that had won or placed second in a couple of tournaments. That team had been picked to win the tournament by many of the coaches. It signaled to us we were doing well. We thought they were undefeated and would be one of the top teams when the those advancing were posted.

When the postings came out most of the teams that were supposed to be represented found themselves advancing. The team we hit round six who was one of the best teams in the tournament did not advance. We felt it quite odd. Once the postings are completed, a coach has the right to examine the record of any competitor who did not advance. Their coach told me they had the wins to go to out or elimination rounds, but while the fifth-round judge had voted for them, she had given them a very low score on speaking points indicating they had been speaking too fast! They were the seventeenth team and had missed out on speaking points.

After all the tournament results showing who was advancing into the elimination rounds were posted, there was an evening full of entertainment, band, dancing, and if you were over twenty-one, some alcoholic drinks. My team had been instructed to only have non-alcoholic beverages. I did not want any hangovers the next morning which might prevent the best performance possible. They also had a curfew of 10:30 p.m. to be back to their rooms and as usual, I would make my nightly check-up at 11:00 p.m. to verify compliance.

Most people would just assume that people competing would not stay out late or drink too much because it would affect their performance the next day, but it was amazing to me how many students were always out at midnight and not in their rooms resting. This was not a vacation, it was a job, and my students were supposed to represent me, the college, and themselves; this was our job at this time. For some of the students this was their social outings and as young men and women, twenty to twenty-four years old, wanted to experiment new situations. Most of the older students had already been there and done such experimentation.

I went to each of the rooms verifying all student compliance had been met. When I got to Terry and DeWayne's room, only Terry was present. After talking with Terry, I went downstairs to the tournament event and found DeWayne sitting with one of the team members that did not advance. He was not just talking. He was drinking. I walked up to the table.

"DeWayne, it is past curfew, and it looks like you are drinking. Would you please come with me back to your room?" I asked now, standing between him and one of the other team members, who seemed to be very intoxicated. DeWayne stood then turned to face me.

"None of these people have curfews. Their coaches let them be adults and make their own decisions about when to go to bed. I like that and as an adult I will no longer abide by your curfew. What do you say about that?" he asked.

"Just because they don't have a curfew does not mean there should not be one. We are not here to party, but rather we are here to do a job that we have been preparing and working toward all year. You are not here by yourself. You are here as a team member and should take into consideration how breaking curfew might negatively affect their outcome if you don't do your best to help the team," I countered.

"Is that right?" he questioned.

"Besides, you are not twenty-one." I said, looking as stern as possible.

"You don't have to be twenty-one in this state to drink. And besides, it's not my job. You're the only one that gets paid. I guess we work for you, but none of us get paid. Guess we are free labor," he said sitting his beer down on the table.

"Your pay is found in the results you obtain, and, in the journey, you enjoy getting there. Your pay is all the meals that people have given to you, the trips you have been provided to libraries so you could spend hours of research at no cost. My making sure you got groceries, trips to the doctor, the little everyday things were your pay. The trips to various exotic tournament locations you have not traveled to, hotels, the meals, and new friends you have, and recognition you get. You cannot perform as well without proper sleep and having no hangover in the morning," I said trying my best to allow him to see himself as a part of a team dynamic that he was an integral part of at this prestigious tournament.

"How about you go back up and get the amount of sleep you need to function at your best, but I will stay here and spend some extra energy with friends who get treated as adults. Are some of them drunk?

Yes!! Are some of them doing weed? Yes, they are! Will those that advanced be there in the morning during the first early round? Again, yes, they will be there, and the tournament will continue. Look at all these people who don't have a curfew. They are adults and can make up their own minds!" DeWayne said sitting back down.

"I am going to turn around and go back up to my room in just a minute. I hope you will go with me. First, each coach can set the rules they want. All of you have signed a tournament representation agreement outlining all acceptable tournament etiquette and expected acceptable behavior recommendations. One last thing, while most of these people are old enough to drink, you are not. You need your rest and besides that your partner is upstairs preparing for tomorrow while you are here taking a break," I told him. I now reached out with open arms for him to go with me.

"I am not going upstairs with you. There really is nothing you can do about me being here missing curfew hours and having any effect on me," he said walking back over to where he was when this conversation started and picked up his beer and took a sip.

"I do have power. If you are not up in your room in ten minutes, I will have you eliminated from the tournament before the elimination rounds begin." I promised. I knew the college would back my decision because it was the best routine, and it was part of the performance contract each student signed prior to leaving and competing in this or any tournament.

"You may have the power, but you won't use it. I have the power now," he said placing his foot on the table where he was sitting.

"Why would you think I won't honor my statement to you?" I asked.

"Because we have worked too hard, and you want to be known as taking a program and making it great so quickly!" He said standing and posturing.

"I have the power, and I will do what is needed. I am not going to argue with you. You are an eighteen-year-old adult and must take responsibility for not following your dream that helps us all." I said as I turned to walk toward the elevators.

"Terry and me made your name this year. You have too much of an ego in all this new talk and recognition. Add all the time you spent investing in the two of us for you to just pull us out; that will never happen," DeWayne said. I turned to face him. At this point I did not care who heard my decree.

"Terry and I would be the correct word choice. I spent that time and effort helping all of us. You signed a contract that outlined what you would do and not do at these tournaments." I spoke. DeWayne was now showing signs of intoxication. He was slurring his words. He was becoming extremely emotional.

"No, you have spent too much time and effort to let something like me drinking a little beer keep "US" from winning," he screamed.

"You have heard what I said, and you can take it at face value."

"No, that is not true and this thing about not being to bed at a prescribed time is bullshit," he said emphasizing each word while at the same time slurring them as many drunks do.

"If you are not in your room in ten minutes, I will have you removed from the tournament and fly you home first thing in the morning because you will no longer be representing our college! I am not looking back. I will have this discussed at our team meeting in the morning." I said moving toward the elevator but wanting to hear back from DeWayne that he would be going up in the elevator with me to his room. I heard only laughter getting stronger instead of weaker each step I took.

"DeWayne, I have won state and national honors. If you don't do this request, you will never be able to make that claim," I said continuing my single, uninterrupted way to the elevator and my room.

When we had our team meeting, all were present except DeWayne. I informed those who did not already know what had happened and asked them what they felt should be done. All, including Terry, wanted me to have him removed from the tournament. Terry would be hurt the most because he needed DeWayne as his partner in the debate category.

"I called Vice President Hurd this morning seeking guidance and was told it was up to me how I wanted to handle the consequences of this infraction. I think it should be a team decision. I will abide by your will with no consequences to anyone voting on the opposite side of the majority," I told my precious group. I wanted them to be a part of the decision, but not be afraid to participate in something that directly impacted their team standing and outcome. I would accept their will.

"I think it should be tossing him from the tournament. He has known all along the consequences of defiance," Terry said. One by one, all of them voiced different reasons but the same outcome. Once the meeting was over, I went down to the tournament headquarters and told the instructors running the debate portion of the tournament I was removing my team. None of them could believe I was instituting such a "radical" reaction.

"If I were you, I would come up with something you can do to punish him after the tournament has ended. You are hurting your entire team. This team might win the entire tournament. They are the top team coming out of the preliminary rounds. As you know, they will be hitting the sixteenth team. Why harm his partner? What did he do to cause this problem? What lesson will that teach all his teammates?" asked the director of debate at the tournament. They did not know I had talked with the team before arriving at the debate headquarters. My team understood team unity and team responsibility. We arrived knowing what the entire team could do if it stayed a team.

"The first thing is he will not be able to say he is a national champion. Some day he will know he missed something he wanted as badly as all of us. His anger got the best of him. What will I teach him if his consequence winds up being that he doesn't go to the celebration the college will be giving us when we get back? I think he will learn the type of behavior he displayed at this tournament is not acceptable. My entire team has made this decision and agree this is the course of action needed." I said with tears in my eyes and a broken heart.

"Are you sure?'" "Yes, do it." I said, turning and walking out of the room.

The rest of my team shortly learned the seventeenth team that they pulled up was the team the boys beat in the sixth preliminary round. In case you were thinking it might have been ReAnne that had given them the low speaking score, it was not her.

I had DeWayne taken to the airport and flew him home that morning. Our team without debate won awards but not as many as we would have done if he had been there with us. Terry always felt we did the right thing even though he didn't get to participate because of the action of his partner.

When we returned home, I had a very nice plaque made for Terry that read, "Top Preliminary Team at the National Finals."

The team pulled up to replace our team, (the seventeenth team) won the tournament. They were the team that many thought would do so when the tournament began. One of the members was the one drinking with DeWayne.

At nationals the next year, the coach from the team that was advanced was talking to one of the other coaches and did not see me nor know I could hear his conversation as he boasted to the other coach the following:

"Last year my team was saved by this newbie coach who had a dispute with one of his debaters about breaking some curfew or drinking a little. These kids are going to do what they want. We are not their parents. Can you believe it, he withdrew from competition the top team in the tournament. What an idiot. Students stay up and drink all the time. For some of them, this is the only time they get to be free from their parents or others!" he declared. He continued laughing.

"You must take all the breaks in life that are given to you. If you're the top team, why on God's earth, would you eliminate the best team so another team could possibly win?" he asked.

I stood up from where I was sitting and walked past the two of them as they continued to speak. I wanted that coach who I no longer admired or respected to be able to point out to his friend that coach who stood up for fairness and who had ethics. Each time I find myself thinking about the lesson learned I know in my heart it was the right choice that needed to be made. It was the correct lesson. Some decisions are difficult to make, but the decision to make them sets some coaches apart from others.

Dewayne taught me that honor, integrity, prestige all come with a price. It is easy to look away from a problem, but society needs us to stand firm on what is right and correct what is wrong. Terry became a college professor and neither of us have heard from DeWayne again.

CHAPTER TEN:
BAKERSFIELD COLLEGE

Homecoming Blues

I was up early Monday morning because I wanted to get an early start on what would be both a day of celebration and one of great sorrow. The forensics team had a celebration dinner planned for Monday evening with special guests who included the students, their parents and family, staff, professors, and administrators. I had invited those I thought would be rewarded for what they had contributed to helping me recruit, allowing the students to practice in front of their classes, assisted with judging at tournaments, and those who bought from our many fundraising projects. I also made it a point to seek out the Academic Senate President and the Faculty Union President.

I also invited administrators ranging from our department chairperson all the way to the college president. I did not want anyone with any type of power to say they had not been invited. I did not have any indication of how many would come, but I had booked the largest conference room in our building. I was told it could accommodate any size function.

What I did not know revealed itself when I opened my office and listened to the messages awaiting my attention. My chair, Dr. Wooton, wanted to meet with me at 10:00 a.m. to discuss the actions I had taken while at the national tournament. I was asked to have a timeline prepared of the events and be ready to address the strategy I took in making sure each of the students knew the protocol, what I had said to DeWayne and Terry before meeting with the other students, and how I had concluded to eliminate DeWayne was the best course of action.

It was 9:00 am and I had class until 10:00 am. I did not have time to prepare in writing what he had requested. I certainly could discuss it from memory but did not have a written document to take to the meeting.

Once I finished my class, I walked back to my office and went directly from there to the departmental office. Dr. Wooten was behind closed doors. His secretary was not at her desk. I could hear the two of them laughing. It was controlled laughter like a joke had been told and someone was being polite. I sat down waiting for them to finish what they were discussing and then when the secretary returned to her desk, she announced I was waiting.

Denna LaRoy, the department secretary, was known by the rest of the faculty to be someone who went above and beyond her job for faculty. If you gave her a task to complete for you, it would be done at the highest level with great professionalism. I had left a handwritten outline of the program for the evening presentation with her before leaving for nationals. I had called and asked her if she wanted me to type it out before I left. She told me to write it out and she would make it perfect. She smiled as the door opened.

"Good morning and good luck!" she said softly as she walked to her desk, picked up a packet of papers and walked back to Dr. Wooten's office. She knocked on the door, opened the door, took the papers into his office, leaving the door open so I could see her hand him the paperwork. She then turned around to me and announced my appointment with the following words,

"Mr. Reel is here at 10:15 for his 10:00 am. meeting."

I was there on time waiting for Dr. Wooton to be available. She stepped aside and I entered. Wooten did not stand to greet me. He sat behind the large wooden desk with a glass top.

"It is nice of you to join us," he said motioning for me to sit in the chair directly in front of him.

"We just got back late last night. I got your message this morning when I arrived at school.

Today is a very hectic day with the celebration for the students and meeting all the press deadlines." I said, wondering why his choice of words and the way the words were delivered indicated he did not mean what was said as a compliment.

"I left that message two days ago. I would have thought you would have arrived early enough today to prepare for what I am sure you know will be happening because of your actions," he responded with a very matter of-fact attitude.

"Each of the students signed the college's pledge of sportsmanship, honesty, and agreement to obey all rules outlined in the travel request mandated by the college prior to leaving for competition." I retorted.

"Well, let's get to the first part of this faculty evaluation." Dr. Wooten said as he opened the folder that Ms. LeRoy had handed him.

"First, if this is an evaluation, shouldn't I have been informed of such?" I asked.

"Since I have visited your classroom three times and you have not been prepared for my visit, I left a voice message two days ago providing ample time to meet the requirements of your contract." he said, now placing several pages down on his desk.

"I was prepared each time. I provided you with a copy of my syllabus so you would know what was happening the day you chose to visit. I told you any day would be acceptable to me because I was not going to change things that were planned," I claimed, but was interrupted.

"I wanted to hear you lecture each time I visited. You were never lecturing. You were not prepared!" he said, raising his voice.

"I was prepared to do what was outlined in the course syllabus. You could have visited any day you wanted. The course syllabus informs when I am lecturing." I responded now raising my voice level to match his.

"My evaluation paperwork shall indicate your unwillingness to lecture when asked," he said now reading from his paperwork.

"Should I stop this interview and get a faculty representative to be here?" I asked.

"The contract stipulates that is one possibility made available to you." he countered.

"I think the contract also states that an official evaluation needs to be identified as such. I don't think this was identified in such manner. However, I have nothing to hide, and will have an opportunity to respond to what you have to say, so let's proceed. It seems to me you have decided to find reasons whether fabricated or not to justify your evaluation. I don't deserve this treatment."

"I want to cover two separate evaluation issues. The first deals with your classroom presentational skills. I have nothing to report on your speaking skills so I will have to indicate it is not to standard." Wooton said, placing the top paper back under the other pages he was holding.

"While I was not officially lecturing, I certainly interacted with the students individually as well as when they were doing small group work. I was certainly talking during your unannounced visits. Was I displaying interactive skills, did I provide good questions, directions, and explanations? Was I kind, caring, compassionate, demanding, too demanding, not demanding enough? Did I answer questions appropriately depending on the situation? Was I inclusive? I think those are the criteria you should address." I suggested.

"I told you after the first visit that I wanted to hear you lecture instead of doing activities. I visited two additional times and neither one provided me an opportunity to hear you lecture and evaluate it. I think this is grounds for such an evaluation you will be given," he claimed ignoring what I said.

"Again, you could have looked at the syllabus and visited during one of the times it indicated to all I would be lecturing. What else are we going to address? Do you need any additional information regarding sending DeWayne home early?" I asked.

"I don't know the issue is sending him home early. It really should be evaluating your decision to remove him from the tournament."

"He broke at least three of the items he signed that he would not do." I said now knowing there would be no fairness.

"What are those issues?" Wooten asked.

"First, was to not consume alcoholic products while at tournaments. Second, he was to be in at curfew time. Third, he was defiant when confronted by me. Should I continue?" I asked.

"I do believe that alcohol consumption age is lower in that state. Curfew is an arbitrary time you have set. As far as being defiant, did he tell you he would not compete? Didn't he say he would be ready to compete?" Dr. Wooton questioned.

"Are you suggesting I should not have held each of the students to the standards this college imposes?"

"I am trying to show you how you could have supported them while at the same time not overreacting with something that brought great consternation from many people in attendance and also to this college," Dr. Wooton claimed, appearing to be on my side but was positioning himself as an adversary.

"I followed proper protocol. I enforced our student travel policy requirement, I provided an opportunity to have the student, after breaking that policy, to continue competing and save face, and even after DeWayne participated in insubordinate behavior, I pleaded one last time for him to resolve the situation; he failed to act in an acceptable manner. I am sure that if you had been there and experienced that behavior from one of our students, you would have done the same thing." I said feeling confident any school administrator would have followed through in a similar manner. I wanted him to finally support what I had been told to enforce was done correctly from an administrative point of view.

"You are wrong. I would have told the student that once we returned, there would be consequences imposed for breaking the governing rules.

I would have left it there and not gone any further and returned to my room." he said, smiling as he took out another piece of paper.

"What consequences would he have faced in that scenario?" I asked.

"One that would not have impacted the college standing at nationals, one that would have not impacted the other student who worked as hard if not harder than he, and one that would have benefited all the other students because the team would have benefited from any ranking the debate team would have earned and those he would have earned in his individual events competition. You sacrificed all when I do not feel it was necessary." Dr. Wooton said, handing me a piece of paper with the title of Reprimand typed at the top.

"This will go in your file. It will be part of your permanent file that will be used in your evaluation at the end of the year regarding retention of your position. You may respond in writing and that answer will also be attached to the file. Now, lastly, I want to share with you your inadequacies when it comes to creating and publishing handouts. I think you probably know how to spell these misspelled words, but haste makes waste," he said handing me the program for the presentation for the students.

The word "dessert" said "desert" and "acknowledge" said acknoledge."

"I did not type this program. Our department secretary told me before I left for nationals, she would type it for me. I wrote it out in hand for her because I didn't have time to finish it." I responded trying to clarify who was responsible for the typos or misspellings.

"I told her to type it as you provided it to her!" he said, smiling and shaking his head.

"Is it not the responsibility of an executive secretary to catch any misspellings?" I asked. I had specifically asked her if I needed to make sure everything was spelled properly before I left for the tournament.

"When she is working for me, yes! When she is doing you a favor, she has been instructed to type what you give her."

"I wish I had known she had two sets of instructions. It appears she has one for you and the other faculty members and a different one for me. If you choose to allow this program to be used at the awards ceremony tonight, it will be a reflection on all of us; and I will point out tonight in a joking way, that the department slipped up and the selfcorrecting spell checker needs some work but that we all love the department secretary," I then smiled.

"She will never do any typing for you if you do something like that," Dr. Wooton said sitting back down.

"I can do my own typing if needed or will hire someone to do it for me. I don't like the game you have chosen to play. I see now you have been brought into the "good old boys club" that has lost sight of what is best for our students but instead, exploits what is best for appearances. By the way, I won't sign that reprimand, so you can put it in my file without me signing it or you can place it anywhere else you choose." I said, now standing preparing to leave the meeting.

"I will be evaluating you again tomorrow and expect to see you lecturing or I will have to make a comment about your continued inability to not be prepared in your ongoing tenure evaluation." Dr.

Wooton said, now smiling even bigger than before and standing.

"Check the syllabus you were provided and see when I am lecturing if that is what you want to see. Visit on one of those days." I responded as I turned and walked out of the office.

The dinner itself went smoothly. The parents in attendance had nothing but praise for the team and the support they thought the college had given. From that point forward, however, the department secretary never reacted to me the same as before this incident. She had been placed in a very tenuous position. She was a subordinate to Dr. Wooton. Her loyalty and job were controlled by him. She too had become part of the toxic atmosphere that placed students second instead of first. I do not blame her for the situation the administration placed her in dealing with faculty. I see her fault was in how she carried out her job. Unless she had been instructed to misspell the words in the program, she could have done the work prior to Dr. Wooton knowing anything about misspelled words.

The celebration for the students started on time that evening. There was ample food, drinks, and desserts. The brochure had desserts misspelled once it was opened to the food section. The student recognition section had some of the student names misspelled also. Finally, the acknowledgement section was also full of misspellings. I waited until it was my turn to speak about our winning team.

"Good evening, ladies and gentlemen, students, staff, faculty members, our department chair Dr. Wooton, our Division Dean, the three attending vice presidents, and of course our very own President Owens, who singlehandedly oversees all the programs at the college. If I take time to personally name all the contributing administrators to our success story, we would still be celebrating way into the night. I have been asked to be brief because so many of our students have won so many awards.

Before we announce those awards, I have just two announcements and the first concerns our beautiful program. If you don't have one,

Dr. Wooton has extra copies. I want to thank our department secretary, Denna LaRoy, for creating the beautiful front cover and typing the program. As we all know, she does a great job and goes above and beyond to make things we give her look professional and first class. Let's give her some special recognition for her efforts." I claimed as loudly as possible. There is a pause because of the applause coming from the group.

"As many of you know, sometimes things just happen. When we leave handwritten notes that must be translated by other people, mistakes take place. When spellcheck does not catch a word, things happen that becomes a mistake. Spellcheck creates interesting interpretations from time to time. This sometimes results in misspelled words. I left handwritten notes for our program before leaving for nationals. If you search the program, a couple of misspelled words can be found in the middle section of the program. I won't blame anyone. Sometimes things just happen, and we must learn to live with it. People are not always perfect. Sometimes errors are made.

If you need to focus on those little areas instead of the real reason we are here tonight, blame me or any administrator. We all have broad shoulders and can take full responsibility for any mistakes. You may be one of the people who only wants to point out all the praises and outstanding accomplishments you are about to hear. One more thing before this love fest begins. We are one less person here tonight than when we left for nationals. That person did not die. He broke the rules and regulations the college established concerning etiquette and behavior. We as a team are expected to follow those guidelines. We sign the agreement committing to such dedication for fairness and conduct behavior. Because of those rules that person was removed from the tournament as called for by our very own administrative guidelines developed for this college under the tutelage of Dr. Owens, our college president. I have taken the liberty of having printed copies of them here tonight. If any of you would like a copy, I have them for you." I said, now walking toward towards to be handed to our students.

"Now, let's get started with what I am calling *A National Celebration for Bakersfield College!*

I spent two years fighting my own chair, Dr. Wooton, and the administration. This type of academic corruption was at every level from staff, faculty, and administration. You played ball with them, or your playing time was limited in duration. I never stopped hearing those words the assistant said regarding Daniel Turner, "We are everywhere,"

This was during the same time I was establishing a very competitive speech team, traveling back and forth to Fresno on weekends when I had no tournaments to continue working at Spenser's Hair Salon, and establishing an ongoing relationship with ReAnne. It was taking a toll on me. I wanted to succeed at my alma mater but did not know at what price I could continue.

By the end of my second year, I was searching for a new position where I prayed students mattered. I gave notice in early March once nationals were over that I would not be returning. By this time, my fight with Dr. Wooton was so widespread, the president of our local teacher's union stopped by my office and encouraged me not to leave, but to fight. He wanted me to become the case against the college that would put the faculty in a position to control their own fate and to no longer allow administrators not to follow proper protocol and procedures when evaluating faculty members.

I was told many faculty members were too weak to fight, but I was young enough and had the best chances to win for all of those who in the past had left, and for those who had stayed to be free from the constant changing consequences of exploitation of certain administrators to cover-up or not report certain academic, counseling, or sports related infractions. I was told it might be a long battle, and I might even be fired, but the union would back me and go to court if needed. He told me I was not the first to encounter an administrative nightmare.

He felt I would be the best candidate because of my participation and academic involvement in many of the student success programs. I had support from the Associated Student Body. He also pointed out my written and oral public announcements to the community made my awareness much greater than other faculty members. He also suggested how my student evaluations could win my opportunity to stay on campus and fight for the students. He wanted me to stay and fight for other faculty, our students, and for myself.

I felt I could win, but some of the students might face crossfire from some of the fallout. The only positive note for me regarding Dr. Wooton and his blatant attempt at sabotage and retaliation came as a silent moment of what he thought was one last jab at me. One of the other faculty members had become very ill. This faculty member was loved by Dr. Wooton. It had not mattered that this person had missed classes that semester, and that I had been secretly invited over to help with grading all the final examination essays for three classes. I sat for hours reading, critiquing, writing positive statements, and suggesting many ways of improving comments on over 100 papers for the ill faculty member.

At the final department meeting, Dr. Wooton went to great lengths to praise this faculty member even saying he had read some of the papers after they were turned into the department secretary and found even in the time of great physical despair, that the faculty member had found the strength to not only correct but make positive suggestions how each student could become a better writer. He had no idea I was the person he was praising.

I learned from Dr. Wooton that it is not enough to be the best one can be when the environment where you work is hostile, threatening, and is not a happy place to spend your working hours. You need to leave and find a place that brings you joy, has purpose, and is a place where you are respected and have respect for those involved in the process of educating students.

CHAPTER ELEVEN: BAKERSFIELD HIGH SCHOOL

Tom Step

The person I was replacing at Bakersfield High School had retired from teaching. He had coached for many years and had relatively good results. My principal told me that the other candidate who had been seriously considered taught in the school district at the junior high school level and that I would have two of his children in my program. He also shared that a parent organization had been formed to raise money to help with travel and these parents also participated at tournaments as judges. When I was given my formal contract and teaching assignment, I was disappointed that there was no class for forensics. Forensics was an entirely extracurricular activity.

My forensics participation was to be seen as part of an assignment in addition to my teaching load.

I suddenly realized why the last coach had retired.

Many of the high-powered high school programs had half or in some instances the entire teaching load in forensics. My schedule was five days per week with seven periods each day. My scheduled looked like this:

Period One	Freshman Grammar
Period Two	Sophomore Writing
Period Three	Sophomore Remedial Reading
Period Four	Sophomore Remedial Reading
Lunch	
Period Five	Junior American Literature
Period Six	Junior American Literature
Period Seven	Prep

I was given the names of students who had participated in forensics in the past. The administration gave me their schedules and instructed me to contact them. The students held food sales on campus to raise funds for travel. We immediately were known as the cool campus food handlers for the speech team.

I was told the school would cover most of the entry fees to compete. My budget was only enough to participate in minimal competition for the entire year.

I knew we would have to go to many more competitions for the students to be totally prepared to win state or national honors.

On the very first day of classes, I learned that before the flag salute, a student would make announcements over the intercom regarding the daily activities like (sports, ASB, dance, scholarship deadlines, and special campus events). There was a flare at the start of the program. Music played and a deep DJ voice said, "This is Tom Step, coming to you from the Driller Radio Station (KBHS) bringing you the news for the day." After this introduction, he went on to share campus wide news. I had read my recruit list and I was happy to see that Step was one of the students I was to follow-up with, who had previously participated in forensics. I was sitting at my desk during my lunch break when the door opened, and a young man entered.

"I take it you are Mr. Reel," he said. I knew this was Tom Step because of his distinct radio professional voice.

"And you must be Tom Step, KBHS DJ," I replied in my attempted radio voice.

"It is only one of my jobs. I am the youngest licensed and professional radio show host at a commercial radio station here in Bakersfield. I have my own show two evenings and one weekend morning. I think I have found my true calling. Well, unless I find that public speaking can lead to something more lucrative." he said smiling.

"Lucrative, is a relative word. I don't know how much this market pays for radio hosts, but there are some markets where a hard-working person can become wealthy. You are the professional radio operator. Is this what you want to do for the rest of your life? Does this make you happy? Have a plan B! College might help. I think you should attend a fouryear college that has a solid reputation in radio broadcasting," I quickly responded waiting to hear if he had college ambitions.

"I was planning to attend Bakersfield College until you left. I am a junior here, so I have two more years to determine what to do. But first, I must get back to the station, so I won't disappoint all my fans, who are enjoying lunch and the music I have chosen for them. I have great influence over each one of them!" he said turning to leave.

"When will you come back to see me?" I asked.

"I can come after school today. We should have about ten students, whom I think would be very competitive this year with the right coaching." he added, going out the door.

"I am sure with the correct combination of students and with me, as the coach, we can make that happen," I yelled as the door closed shut. He said something as he went down the hall singing a song of joy. I could hear it from my classroom. I wanted him to hear that there would be a combination that included him and me making the choices for him to succeed.

Tom quickly became one of my favorite students, although he earned subpar grades in most of his classes. With additional time spent on his work, he could have been a straight "A" student. He was bright, witty, and talented.

He had started his radio DJ work as a hobby and had begged the staff and the DJ's at the commercial station to teach him the trade. He was persistent and persuasive. He completed all his training, took all the tests, completed the mandatory hours, and was the youngest person licensed at the Bakersfield station or in any commercial radio station in California. He picked up extra work for his own spending money. He wanted to be self-supportive to take the burden away from his parents.

Tom and his debate partner, Tiffany, became one of my top two debate teams. Depending on the tournament, either one would rank slightly higher than the other. His partner was a junior like him, but my other team was composed of two seniors. None of my students were allowed to compete in just one event. In regular speech competitions Tom also did impromptu speaking. He was very good at this event because of all the things he had read and his ability to talk about many things on his radio shows.

Both teams often made it to the elimination rounds. The seniors lost in the semi-finals to the team Tom and Tiffany would be facing in the finals. The national qualifying tournament was only a few weeks away from the state finals. Most of the juniors and seniors knew how stressful this home stretch was like. Only one team would make it. You had to win at either the national qualifying tournament or be the state winner to go to the nationals. I went to see Tom and Tiffany before the final round started. It was important to talk to them about why they were in the finals.

"I want both of you to enjoy this minute. I know debate is not what you want to be known for, but it will show all the other schools that two persuasive speakers can get the job done also!

"They are from West High and will just cream us. It might be humiliating. Why don't we just forfeit the round?" Tom asked. His partner looked at him in shock.

"Those two spoiled rich boys only know how to do one thing, and that is to read as fast as they can when presenting materials their coach prepared. I don't think either one of them can think on their feet," Tiffany said as only she could while putting Tom in place. Tiffany wanted Tom to see he was not the only person who had an opportunity to advance and earn a ticket to nationals. She continued, "You are right.

Why don't we walk into that room, put all our materials out, wait for the room to fill, and then just say, 'Sorry people,' we should have never made it this far, and our opponents are so good, we just want to give up and we are sorry we inconvenienced you and all the judges and teams we beat. We are sorry the judges got it wrong, and all you should have won, and we would like to have those rounds reversed because we are losers! Is that what you think and want Tom? Do you really think this team we are about to hit cares what we are thinking? I think they are scared to death they must face us. We did not get here by chance. We beat exceptional teams. Our practice sessions and strategy for this tournament has paid off for us. We finally have the coaching we have wanted, and you want to quit? You think we should just give up? You want me to give up my dream? I have heard you talk about going to nationals since we started debating. It is now one round away from happening and you want us to just give up? Really? I bet they are scared because they know they can't read as fast as possible and throw out so many arguments that can't humanly be answered because they are going to have to be persuasive and don't know how to do it!" She said knowing her reverse psychology would work.

I thought it was time I brought both of them back to reality because they had won and beat all those other teams because they were powerful speakers and had the evidence to support their positions which made them very dangerous in local competitions when the lay judge wanted persuasive speaking that contained examples, easily understood concepts, and logically moved from one point to another.

"Really, you think that is an acceptable solution to the great honor you have obtained in getting to the final round. Just give up. Let the other team not even have to deal with the most persuasive two debaters they will face? Do what you do best. Make them debate on your terms. You control the debate. Tell the judges you are going to talk with them and group like arguments together and not respond to each separate argument that does not need to be addressed and would force you to talk so fast they could not understand you. Make them debate you!" I said, trying to be calm and to inspire them.

"Do you think we belong here?" Tiffany asked.

"Of course, I do. You had to debate six preliminary rounds and three additional rounds of the best teams in our region to arrive where you are right now. You must be doing something right. I think the judges at this tournament are sending a message to the debate community they want ethos, pathos, and logos," I said as they looked at each other and then quickly back to me with quizzical expressions.

"Credibility, emotion, and logic; didn't you learn anything from my debate lectures?" I asked.

"Oh, of course. I guess we did, or we would not be here representing you," they both said almost in unison.

"You are representing me, the school, but most importantly yourselves. Besides you are a much prettier team. Well one of you," I said smiling.

"You have to forgive my partner she tries to look pretty," Tom said, smiling and reaching over to take Tiffany's hand.

"I don't think anyone would mistake the prettier person Mr. Step. Now let's get this done," I said loudly and proudly.

I did not share with them that some of the coaches felt they should not have been in that round. They added additional judges to make sure it was a "legitimate" decision. Some of the coaches favored the movement away from using persuasion to one of asserting as many arguments as one could read and talk about 400 to 500 words per minute. Yelling is a good way to describe such debating.

What those coaches did not understand was the persuasiveness of this team. We debated the other team. Both opponent's mis-analyzed this team from the beginning of the debate.

They talked fast and ignored our instructions to examine key arguments only and to look at the strength of those positions from real life examples or to examine expertise information to reveal real world examples of what has been tried that is similar and the impact it has had. Both Tom and Tiffany were very effective during their cross-examination times. They pressed them to prove the assertions that only their evidence suggested might help. They were calm, courteous, and asked questions that had to be answered yes or no by the other team.

When we got to the awards, the director (who felt his team should have won the tournament) and whose team had lost to us in the semi-final round was very upset. This coach and teacher were supposed to announce the decision but would not do so; he walked out of the building and left the school. He was so upset he did not attend the assembly with his students. The tournament director had someone else announce the results. An individual events coach was recruited to read the results of the final round.

We won and were going to the National Forensics League (NFL) tournament in Portland. When we got to the national tournament, Tom's partner, Tiffany, became very ill and was hospitalized before the end of the preliminary rounds. She wound up having to stay an additional six days after the tournament ended before she was well enough to return home.

Tom entered the Kiwanis speech contest because it was giving scholarship awards to winners as the levels increased. He won the first two levels and the next level that was giving several thousands of dollars in scholarships, was being held at Fresno
State.

He had met a competitor from Clovis High and they had become friends. When I went to pick Tom up at his home to drive to Fresno, he shared with me that he had been talking with his friend who was driving his own car to the contest that he would be driving a new two-seater sports car and they would meet in the parking lot.

"You told him you owned a new car?" I asked.

"I never told him it was mine," he said trying to justify the vague position.

"Did you say it was my car we would be arriving in for the contest?" I asked as straight forward as possible.

"I don't remember using those words," he responded knowing he had deliberately not clarified the accuracy of the conversation.

"Why? What is wrong going in my car?" I asked, wanting to know the more important answer as to what was going on with Tom. He was usually a down-to-earth person who took great pride in watching out for others and the last person to hurt the feelings of anyone.

"All of those kids from Clovis, or Hoover, or even Bullard drive their own new cars. I don't even have an old one. I can't ask my mom to help me. Besides her car is too old. What do you say?" he asked in a coaching manner. I thought for a minute before replying to what was now a touchy point.

"What happens if they want you to come back or go someplace?" I asked like I imagined a parent would when trying to get to the bottom of something that should never have taken place.

"If you let me drive into the parking lot, I will tell them I couldn't bring my car, but you let me drive your car. How is that?" he requested in a playful mood smiling.

"That is better."

"Technically, my mom's car will become mine sometime in the future." Tom proclaimed.

"Do you plan to take that car to college?

"If I were a betting man, I would say the answer to that question is a resounding NO!" he responded.

"Well, as long as you tell them I allowed you to drive my car, I guess it is alright." I responded and pulled over to switch drivers.

"I didn't want to do it until right before we got to the college," Tom quickly replied.

"Let's do it now so you know how to drive this car. I don't want you hitting something because you have not gotten accustomed to the car before the show-and-tell-time." I said now smiling.

"Pull this fine car over and let a man who can master anything do his thing," Tom commanded. While he did not win, he placed high enough to have some financial aid provided to him for college.

I also introduced him to Dr. Hal Bochin, my coach, who was helping with forensics again for a short emergency time. It was nice to see Dr. Bochin.

Tom wound up attending Fresno State. Dr. Bochin got him a book scholarship just like he had done for me. He also helped him with a grant. He and his friend from Clovis became very competitive just like Bob Vartabedian and I had done for Fresno. They had become close friends.

His junior year at Fresno State, Tom won first place in the United States in Informative Speaking with a speech on *"Spontaneous Human Combustion."* He won the award he had wanted!

Once again, Dr. Bochin had inspired and assisted a student who had great talent to become a superb speaker. The choice of topic and the ability to deliver the message won!

I always felt honored that I was the first, and my student, was the second national champion in the history of Fresno State forensics. Again, a student from the agricultural fields of California was able to grow into a man of honor and integrity. Tom graduated and became a teacher and football coach at a private school where I was principal for a couple of years. Once he finished his certified credential, Tom left the private school and became a public high school teacher in the Los Angeles area. I learned from Tom that a teacher needs to inspire students to do more than they think possible. He taught me that motivation matters. He is still encouraging and inspiring those students who want to become successful. He is a true inspiration, and I am proud of him. I have always had a special place in my heart for Tom and all the accomplishments he has earned and for all those students he has mentored.

CHAPTER TWELVE: BAKERSFIELD HIGH SCHOOL

Xin Liu

The first day of my freshman year grammar class, I met a special student who would win the hearts of many for her talent and dedication. She also possessed one of the best work ethics I have ever encountered. I was taking roll when I called out, "Zin Lie...Lieyou... are you here?

"It is pronounced Shin Lew," she said, as though I was another American teacher mispronouncing her name.

"I am so sorry. I am going to write it down on my roster phonetically, so I won't mispronounce it from this point forward," I promised in my most apologetic voice. As I looked at her, she almost took my breath away. She was extremely attractive, long beautiful black hair, and her voice spoke the English language better than anyone else in class.

"We hear you are the new speech coach. Is that accurate?" she asked.

"I am guilty. I know some people call it forensics," I said preparing to explain why it is so named.

"Yes, some of my friends might confuse it with the activity associated with law enforcement, but I learned the different usages when I was in the sixth grade," she said proudly.

"Do you already have a college degree, or are you here as a faculty member already beginning my evaluation process?" I asked with a big smile.

"No, when I arrived in this country from China, none of my family could speak any English. My parents have taught me and my sister to strive to be the best in all we do. They have sacrificed everything for us since we were starting school and unable to speak English.

We have overcome so much to be where we are now. I have been fortunate enough to have had teachers who have helped me, and I am so very full of gratitude. I want to do extemporaneous speaking.

and would like to learn to debate. I want to attend Harvard or Stanford and feel it will give me an edge when those schools are making their decisions as to who gets into such prestigious schools. "

Xin started in the novice division in both events. She advanced to the junior division after her first tournament in extemporaneous speaking. By the end of her first semester, she was entering and going to the final rounds at most tournaments in extemporaneous. I had paired her with a freshman male as debate partners. They also had moved from novice to junior division in debate. I was very proud of their progress. As a debate team, she and her partner were ranked as the best freshman team and would be challenging any of the returning debaters for senior level traveling squad during their second year. She knew what she wanted and found an opportunity to find out how to make it happen. She was motivated.

At the conclusion of her freshman year, Xin introduced me to her parents and told me how proud she was of her parents and how protective they were of her. They needed to trust me with any traveling overnight trips. I went to meet them at the grocery store they owned. I arrived just a few minutes early as instructed by Xin. She told me her parents thought much was told by punctuality.

"Mom, Dad, this is Mr. Reel. He is our speech coach and is helping me be very successful in developing my speaking skills. He listens to my speeches. He also guides me by critiquing my speeches to make them stronger and more likely to be accepted as being the best by the judges." she said, waiting for them to recognize me.

"We have heard so much about you," Mrs. Liu said.

"We love people who can help our daughter,"

her father revealed.

"The pleasure is always mine. You must be very proud of your daughter; I know I am proud too. I have never met a student who works harder, is willing to listen to what is said, and can understand how to connect these elements.

"We like to hear that because we have taught her to listen and obey teachers always," said Xin's mom.

"You have done a wonderful job of giving your daughter opportunities to succeed. Next year will be the hardest year for us to make advancements for Xin. She will be competing against students from very successful public schools and from very prestigious private schools," I said. Before I could continue, Mr. Liu said,

"She has told us she must compete against students who have been doing this longer and those that are older. Do you think she has a chance?" he asked and stopped talking to hear my answer.

"I think if we can practice as much as needed, and we can travel to the large tournaments away from Bakersfield, she will earn a spot and have a chance to be very successful." I promised. Again, before I could continue, her mom asked,

"How much will this cost?"

"Between what the school is going to contribute, and what the booster club will add, the cost should be minimal," I quickly responded. I did not want them to think they would have to pay too much of their well-earned income for speech competitions.

"Will it be more than a couple thousand dollars?" asked Mrs. Liu, waiting again to hear my answer.

"I am sure it won't be that much!" I responded.

"We think that will be acceptable. We see it as an investment in her education," Mr. Liu said. He took his wife's hand and they immediately walked out of the room.

"I guess you will have me another year," said Xin smiling with joy. Her plan to have me meet her parents had paid off greatly. Both parents were on board with her doing forensics in a most exciting way.

"I really do think you have a chance to go to nationals next year if we can get you to the right tournaments, so you learn from the best!" I spoke in a louder voice so she could hear me as she was closing the door. I was delighted Xin would be returning.

Xin did become a star. She attended nationals the next year at Northwestern University. Not only was she mastering debate, her impromptu and extemporaneous speaking was far superior to anyone in the valley. In fact, there was another female from the Fresno area who had won the national qualifier the last three years, and all thought she would win again. At the national trials, Xin took first place. She was gracious and humble.

She was going to nationals as a sophomore. Xin's parents insisted her younger sister (four years younger) attend with her. Her parents paid all her expenses for her sister. They called her the chaperone. I always thought the real reason her parents insisted her younger sister go with her was so she too could experience something that would motivate her to pursue public speaking. Xin made it to the semifinals. She just missed going to the finals.

Xin taught me that my culture was only one of many cultures that exist within any community. She and her family reaffirmed that hard work and diligence can and does make a difference. I saw firsthand that sacrifices and priorities from parents can make the difference when it comes to their children. Xin was a minority female who understood it was needed and acceptable to be as competitive if not more in an event largely populated by boys. She taught me that grace, compassion, understanding, and perseverance will win. Had I stayed another year, I have no doubt she would have returned and possibly won nationals.

CHAPTER THIRTEEN: BAKERSFIELD HIGH SCHOOL

Nate Moton

I did not feel good about the part of my teaching load which consisted of the two classes of sophomore remedial reading. These students were all reading below third-grade level. Immediately, I knew why they were failing their other courses. They did not know how to read the required novels, the math books, the science books; well, they could not read any of these books that were required in their classes. I asked the principal for the teacher's edition of the book I was to use. I found out there was no such book. This was a new program, and it was up to me to create a curriculum to fit the class.

I talked with a couple of my friends who taught elementary school. When they heard about my situation, they sent me some workbooks that included how to teach consonant and vowel recognition. I went to the public library and shared my task with the librarians, and asked if I could borrow some reading age-appropriate (second/third grade) books. I especially wanted Dr. Seuss books. I created two large boxes that looked like chests to house the books the library allowed me to check-out for the entire semester. I knew I had to begin teaching reading as though the students were back in second grade.

I will never forget the first day of my remedial class. It taught me a lot! The class was full. It was almost equally divided with, perhaps, a slight majority of male students. Most all the students were migrant children who worked in the fields helping their parents. I took roll that first day, and then shared some personal things about myself.

"Good morning, everyone. I know many of you are not happy because you have been forced to take this class. There is a reason why you have been placed in my class. You have been given an unfair education thus far. Let me begin by telling you it is not your fault you find yourself where you are today. Our educational system has let you down. Teachers let you down. Administrators let you down. I won't let you down. You have, for some reason, been allowed to be passed along each grade without someone taking the time and effort it takes to help you become successful in your other classes by knowing how to read at a specific grade level.

I know what it is like to travel the crops; my parents and my brothers and sisters picked oranges in McFarland, beets in Delano, grapes in Shafter, cotton in Buttonwillow, and of course potatoes in Bakersfield. Only one of my older six brothers and sisters graduated from high school. You have a problem! You cannot read at the level you need to pass your classes! You can decide to do something about this, or you can choose not to learn. When that door closes, and this class starts, you can rest assured none of the other students outside of our class will know what we are doing in this class; that is, if you will allow me to teach you what should have been done many years ago. You will see a drastic change in your high school experience if you participate and become involved in this class." I said looking around to see if any of these students wanted to try.

A couple of students were looking down, a few were talking among themselves, but most were looking up and I saw in their eyes that they were reaching out for me to help them.

"So, what makes you think you can do something with us that none of the other teachers could do?" ask a young woman in row three, seat two.

"Because I was like you. I had to develop two different vocabularies. One vocabulary for school, and the other for home. If I did it, I know you can do it. None of my family used proper grammar. If I came home and used two or three syllable words or correct subject verb agreement, family members would say I was trying to fit in with the rich kids. I was simply trying to learn enough so I didn't have to work in the agricultural fields for the rest of my life. I will take all the time that is needed, and we will learn some rules about reading together. There is no book the school district has for us to use. I have been asked to create my own materials for our class. I need your help! This is an attempt to make each of you special and recognized as achievers if we do this together and you take advantage of what is being given to you. This class is what the district calls *An Experimental Program*, and I am being tested as a teacher to see if I am worthy of retaining my job, and you are being tested to see if there is a way you can read well enough to understand the books you must use in your other classes. I want us both to pass. Here you will be given the choice of choosing a book you want to read; and if someone sees that book when you are outside of this class, you say proudly that you have been required to write a children's book and the book you have is an example of the book you have to write. Don't say anything else.

I promise you they will be envious of you. No other class is going to offer such an assignment. It is creative, and you will hold all the power over them. Remember words are powerful, and sometimes we allow them to hurt us. Words are only as powerful as you allow. I used to get my feelings hurt when people called me an *Okie*. Once I stopped allowing that word to have a negative impact on how I responded, it was no longer any fun for those bullies to use. Every single person in this class can be successful if you try. I promise you I will not let you down!" I said now, seeing most of them sitting up at their desks ready to try to learn to read.

"Remember, words are powerful, and sometimes we allow them to hurt us," said someone from the back. It sounded like I was talking. Most of the students turned around because whoever was speaking sounded just like me.

"I want you to remember that sentence. You can be powerful when you read and understand words. Let me give you an example, one of my favorite characters in Dr. Seuss' *Horton Hears a Who* says, 'I sat, and I sat, and I sat!'" I said in the deepest and most animated voice I could produce as I moved toward the back of the class.

"I sat, and I sat, and I sat!" repeated the young man in row four seat seven. I stopped and just smiled in amazement.

"You sound just like me!" I spoke.

"You sound just like me!" he repeated.

"Oh no, I too am from London my son," I said in my best British voice.

"On no, I am from London my dear chap," he said in a better British voice.

"Well, I see you can parrot other's voices, but do you want to learn to read?" I asked standing next to him as I looked down at his seat.

"I can match any voice I hear; and if you tell me a story, I can recite it back word for word!" he exclaimed.

"That is an amazing talent! But the question is can you read those same words? Now, we must continue our class today to help all of you become better readers." I said moving back toward the front of the class.

"Let's get started!" I cried out wanting each one to begin his or her journey of overcoming a huge obstacle in their life. Nate led the charge with humor, wit, and excitement that an adult was going to teach him.

By the end of that class, I felt I could help a certain student become a success immediately by joining our speech team and participating in an event called program reading! As the students left, I asked Nate to stay for just a minute.

"Am I in trouble for what I said in class today?" he asked.

"No. Your life is about to change in a way you cannot imagine," I said while he was walking toward me.

"It won't take much to change my life. What do you have instore for me to do?" Nate questioned.

"You are so good with voices, I thought we would put you into a contest in the category of programmed reading. You take a cutting from a novel or short story, and then tell the story with the narration and voices. It is a reading contest." I said smiling at him.

"But I don't read so good," Nate said somewhat apologetic.

"You have almost a photographic memory and can tell a story in such a manner that not one person will know that you are not reading the story. If fact, you will be sharing every single word as it was written. Reading doesn't get much better for an audience than that." I replied.

"What am I going to share, one of your Dr. Seuss books? I can do all those voices!" he gladly shared, now excited about being able to do something that would give him some self-confidence and do some ego building.

"I am thinking we might do something that is more dramatic and might present a story that has many different levels of suspense. Some parts will be humorous, which is your specialty. It will need to be more than just voices. I also want the story you tell that is a real-life story to have some other levels that will expose tragedy attached to it." I shared trying to move him away from Dr. Seuss. He would use Dr. Seuss to learn to read but would read a far superior book to a willing audience soon. He would succeed. I mean there is nothing wrong with Dr. Seuss, and if it were a contest for children's literature, he would be my main person for you to read.

"I do know tragedy." He quickly responded.

"Why do you say that?" I questioned.

"Well, we don't ever have enough money, and our cars are always breaking down, and the places we live are not the best. At least we stopped moving with each crop. We now drive to those locations. Mom's felt I would do better in school if we lived in a bigger city cause they got better teachers." he explained as he quickly finished before leaving to go to his next class. "Come by after school if you have a couple of minutes." I yelled.

"Tomorrow morning before school will be better. The bus gets here early but leaves just after school is let out. Hope you will be here early so we can talk!" were the last words I heard as the door slammed.

I knew there was a later busing schedule for athletes and students who were involved with other extra-curricular activities. Nate did not know about that bus schedule because he had never participated in such programs. The very next morning exactly thirty minutes before school started, Nate arrived at my classroom. We started talking when he noticed a few other students arriving and beginning working on their projects.

"Boy, this looks like a lotta stuff goin' on in here in the morning. I thought it would be quiet and we might talk about what you said yesterday. Can you explain it more to me?" he asked sitting in the chair beside my desk.

"First, let me say I don't think you cannot learn to read. The level of your understanding and comprehension of words that are needed to read is the problem you are having in school. You know many more words. Because you can't read, you don't recognize them when they appear on paper.

We can take care of the lack of training to read by doing what I am going to be asking you to do during that class. We are going to learn how to read and use consonants and vowels. The activity I want you to join is our competition speech team. It is like a football or baseball team, but the students give speeches and make oral presentations," I explained.

Before I could continue, he commented on what he thought the activity was and wanted specific clarification.

"You mean do things with the brainiacs that don't think people like me are in their same league? Mr. Reel, how do you think I could fit in? I don't have store bought clothes or even really-good-lookin' shoes!" he commented and paused to hear my response.

"I guess I think you can become one of those brainiacs. I am using that word in its most flattering connotation. All those kids are just like you. A couple of them are athletes. Most are not. All students deserve to find a place to excel and feel they are special. We all need to be given praise. Me too! I think you can do this." I proclaimed. I wanted to continue talking but once again was cut off.

"I don't always know what words you are using, but I think I get most of them. Are you sayin' you think I might have what it takes to run with the brainiacs?" he asked smiling.

"I think your spoken language is greater and much better than your written vocabulary. Because you understand more words when you hear them than when you see them in print and are forced to try and determine what they mean limits your understanding. We just need to teach you how to sound out the words, so you hear yourself read the words?" I explained.

"I guess. I can follow words and usually know what they mean when hearing them, but can't spell, so I can't read 'em. I can remember what somebody says, so I can repeat those words if I need to." Nate spoke in an almost whispered manner.

"Never apologize for not knowing something you have not been taught. We only know today what we have been taught earlier. That does not mean we can't learn it today or tomorrow. You think you might want to try this activity? I will be with you every step of the way. I also know the students in our group will accept you and will help you also. What about your parents, they must be on board. Will they be supportive?" I asked hoping the answer would be affirmative.

"I won't ever apologize again for what I don't know. I am constantly trying to improve and find out things on my own. I am friendly and pretty good looking too. My parents won't care what I do cause they know I won't do anything that will get me in trouble," he declared as if he were a person interviewing for a job. I was doing my best to recruit him.

"By the way, there is a second bus schedule to various parts of the city used for students who choose to participate in after-school activities. That bus leaves at 4:30 pm for students participating in various activities for school. You won't have to leave right when the bell rings." I shared trying to help him make his decision.

"Sometimes, I must go to work early in the mornings with my family. I know I can get a couple days a week off if really needed. My Mom's wants me to better myself. She will run interference for me," Nate responded.

"Again, nice vocabulary. We must complete two things. First, we need to find you a cutting to use for competition. Second, we will have to find you some dressier clothes to wear outside of what you usually wear to class for your forensics attire." I said wondering if he knew what a couple of the words meant.

"You must find the story, read it to me, do the voices and I will remember it and do the voices even better. Just kiddin!! The clothes might be more touch and go. I personally don't have any nicer clothes than the ones I wear to school. I do have relatives that dress better than me. I will call them. I can shine my shoes up, but I will have to ask around to my cousins to see if any of them has nicer pants, maybe a sweater, and a nice shirt to wear. You do your part, and I will take care of my part the best I can!" he promised.

I spent the next couple of days researching what might be relevant, slightly controversial, and provide a story needing to be told. There was an exciting comic and civil rights activist, Dick Gregory, who had a memoir out that was getting great reviews and selling a bunch of copies. I got a copy, spent time finding what I thought would be a great cutting, and presented it to Nate. I read it to him doing what I thought would win many awards if those voices could be mastered. At the end, he looked at me with a twinkle in his eye, but also some confusion in his appearance and eyebrows raised.

"How do I respond? I like the story and it definitely needs to be told. Most of your voices were interesting and was' clear and easy to understand. I think we can make it work. There is one big problem. What I cannot do is to say the title of the book. I just won't." He said putting his notes that served as his critique of me down on the desk.

"You have to give both the title and the author before you begin." I said reinforcing the rules for program reading.

"I can't say the title. I won't. That word is not a word I want said about me and I aint' goin' say it in public. Not goin' to come from my lips." he said very convincingly and standing up for his rights.

"Well, how can we be creative and tell the audience the title of the book? What if we were to spell it out? That might have even a greater impact on the audience."

"That might be better. If I spell it, most my relatives won't know the word cause they can't read better than me," Nate said trying to find a way he felt he could comply with the rules and regulations but stand on his own self-worth.

"N-I-G-G-E-R by Dick Gregory," Nate said loudly and proudly.

"The only other thing is we must type a copy of the reading and put it into a binder, and you read from that copy. We will also have to submit a copy to the state and national tournaments when we register for those competitions so we can prove it is an accurate selection from that copyrighted piece of literature," I said, moving closer to him to shake his hand because we were about to have a deal.

"We both know I am not going to be reading it. I will be performing it. You will have to do the other things." Nate quickly responded.

"All the students who perform have it memorized by the time they get to major competitions, so we will be fine. I will have the correct submissions for any tournaments requesting them. So, let's get started." I said shaking his hand.

I placed Nate in the novice division at our local tournament. He came in first place. Most of the judges commented on how superior he was to the other students in style, presence, reading ability, and presentation. They called him an excellent reader.

He quickly moved from novice to junior and then to senior division. At one tournament, I got to see him in the final round. He was clearly the best presenter. The one problem he had was his binder was turned upside down all during the presentation, I kept wondering if anyone else had caught that detail. It did not phase the judges because he won the tournament. However, I did place little arrows on the outside pointing upwards so that did not happen again. Nate, the student who at the beginning of the year could not read much, became the California State Champion in Program Reading.

The high school was very impressed that the students in the two remedial reading classes far exceeded their expectations. At the end of the year, they went from sophomores reading at the secondgrade level to juniors reading at the eighth-grade level. While the district thought the results amazing, I still recognized that they were behind their peers, but no additional reading course was ever required by the district for them.

Nate taught me to continue my dream of helping students who found themselves in similar situations to where I had found myself when

I was attending high school. I became the teacher who had reached out to me. I saw in Nate something he could not see because he had not been given the vision, a mirror, or the stability of having someone be his champion. No other teacher had shown him the love, care, and understanding every single student deserves. He taught me to examine each of my students and to reach out to see if they wanted someone to be an advocate for them.

CHAPTER FOURTEEN:
BAKERSFIELD HIGH SCHOOL

Sarah Bailey

During the summer after my second-year teaching at the school where I had graduated, but from the adult school program, I felt I had provided an example for those who had come after me and were not able to make it out academically.

I was asked if I would like to teach at the Georgetown and Redlands Summer Institutes. When I was at Georgetown, one of the coaches had a student doing a program from a new choreopoem that had just been published and was the hottest new Broadway triumph entitled, *For Colored Girls Who Have Considered Suicide/When the Rainbow Is Enuf,* by Ntozake Shange. I did not like the cutting as presented at the institute but thought I would get a copy of the choreopoem and see if I could do a better job of editing the story of seven girls who had experienced racism, body shaming, rape, and find a better way of telling the story to meet the needs of high school dramatic interpretation when only one person could perform. I had several young girls from the team I thought would be great doing this project.

I felt the new cutting was a superior cutting for use in high school competition.

I surprised myself with the new cutting. My cutting with my editing and merging the seven characters into one; and taking the perspective of having the story told by a third person to first person became an immediate success in my world of coaching. The audience usually gasped or cried when they heard the last four words from the young girl telling the story. I ran my cut version by three of my students who had done well in dramatic interpretation, but none wanted to use the cutting. For one reason or another, they felt the story was too dark, too hopeless, or too extreme. Each one of them felt they wanted to tell a different story rather than to talk about why one would consider suicide. I knew this was a story that needed to be told, but it had to be with someone that could see the desperation, the depletion of self-worth, the tragedy of allowing a person to manipulate someone to the point where a mother was unable to do anything even if the father of her child was to kill her baby while she sat idly by and did nothing. The thought of watching this happen was horrific.

One morning while taking roll in my freshman English class, I called the name of one of my students who was absent. I called it a second time because there was no answer. For some reason, I could not picture the student. The next day as I called roll, I heard a faint "Present," reply when I called the name. I looked up and saw a very shy, reclusive, almost invisible young woman sitting halfway down row three. I had allowed her to sit in my class for two weeks and had not given her the time she deserved from me to give her an opportunity to be part of the class as an active participant. I stopped taking roll. I looked directly into her eyes.

"Sarah Bailey, I am so glad you are in class today. I missed you yesterday. Did you miss us yesterday?" I asked, hoping she would respond.

"As a matter of fact, I did," she responded in a very delicate, breathy, barely audible voice. She also smiled like an innocent child at the end of that statement. I saw innocence at its very core. I saw wisdom and courage that had not blossomed.

I could tell it took some work on her part to muster the will to speak up in a class full of other students.

"Our class is better off today because you are here. I bet you completed your work even though you were not in class. Am I correct?"

I needed her to tell the class she had completed it and it helped prepare her for what was going to take place in class. I wanted them engaged. I wanted them to see homework was not punishment.

"I don't know that is the case, but this is my favorite class. It is amazing to see how easy it is to construct sentences when we apply the rules you are providing for us to use. Wish I had been taught this before getting into high school," she said, ending her sentence quickly and not wanting to occupy too much time to our discussion. She made her point but did not want to occupy too much time in the spotlight.

She wanted me to know she was prepared and ready to respond if I would just force her to participate. She was ready to be forced out of her comfort zone into academic competition.

"I hope this class becomes the favorite class for many of you this semester. Learning how to express yourself in written form in my opinion is the second most important thing one can learn," I said hoping she or someone else would ask what I thought was the most important.

"I always do my homework each night because

I know it teaches us how to apply the rules and suggestions you provide during each class. Now what is the most important thing we can learn besides writing?" she asked.

"I feel that public speaking is the number one means of expression. We take words whether they are written or created live, and we share them so others can hear them instead of reading them. When we do that effectively, that is the most powerful means we must communicate with others," I told them.

"I agree!" Sarah said loudly.

"Now, let's get to work so all of you can understand that subject, verb, objective writing is easy and will help us learn how to make exciting sentences into different types of sentence structures like compound sentences which is our topic today." I shared. I immediately concluded taking roll and went into my lecture for the day. The next few days I paid particular attention to Sarah.

She suddenly became an active participant. I started paying more attention to her writings she completed as homework. I made sure to compliment her on doing so well. She was very expressive, and her choice of words was superior to freshman level writing. It was now Friday, and I would not see this class or Sarah until Monday. I wanted to ask Sarah to observe an upcoming competition.

We were going to attend our first speech competition and I did not have anyone who wanted to perform the cutting I knew would be very powerful.

"Sarah, may I see for just a minute?" I asked as the class was leaving me and heading to their second period class.

"Mr. Reel, did I do or say anything wrong today?" she asked.

"No, of course not. As you know from my discussions in class, I coach the speech team, and this weekend at Fruitvale High School there will be a contest. One of the events is Dramatic Interpretation. I think you would be great in that type of competition. Is there any way you could get there and go see a couple of rounds?" I asked the person I thought might become my next star.

"I don't have any plans for tomorrow. I can ask my mom to take me. Where do I go and how will I know what to go see?" she quickly asked.

"The tournament is being run out of the cafeteria. Show up at 8:30 a.m. and I will meet you. I will introduce you to one of our own girls competing in that event and you can go to her rounds with her and watch some of Bakersfield's finest dramatic interpretation artists. Pay special attention to how the students portray their characters, the different voices they produce for various people they are supposed to be; but most of all pay attention to how they make you feel by the end of performance. I will see you in the morning!" I concluded, secretly praying she would show up and enjoy the activity.

"Ok, see you in the morning," Sarah spoke with excitement and enthusiasm.

The next morning at exactly 8:30 a.m. I walked into the cafeteria at Fruitvale High School and saw Sarah and a grown woman both smiling and waving at me.

"Good morning, Sarah," I said approaching her from across the room.

"Good morning, Mr. Reel. Thank you for this opportunity. I would like to introduce you to a very special person. Mr. Reel, this is my mom Audrey," she responded.

"It is a pleasure to meet you Mrs. Bailey. Your daughter is a delight to have in my class, and I have a feeling she could compete in the activity I want her to watch today. Let me introduce both of you to one of our senior students who is competing in this activity today." I explained, while at the same time, finding and motioning for Evelyn to come and join us.

I had earlier asked her permission to have Sarah go to each of her rounds. I also asked her to share with her the proper etiquette for watching and to explain to her the rules of the event as the day progressed.

Sarah and Mrs. Bailey soon left to shadow Evelyn for that day. I caught up with them at the conclusion of the three preliminary rounds just before postings for the elimination rounds were revealed.

"What did you think?" I asked as I approached all of them and a couple additional members of our team who were discussing those performances and the students, they thought extremely talented. It was encouraging to see how quickly the girls had bonded. It looked like Sarah was delighted she had come.

"Oh my God, it is like watching professional actors. They are all so great. Especially, Evelyn, she should be in Hollywood," Sarah burst out with no intimidation, no fear of being heard, no holding back or expressing how she felt. She was a person who suddenly lit up as she spoke. I was about to speak when Sarah's mom came over to join us.

"Mr. Reel, this is exactly the type of activity we have been trying to find for her since she was about seven years old. She can play almost any character she sees on television for us at home. I think she should join right now! Also, in my humble opinion, Ms. Evelyn should have won every one of those rounds we watched." she declared.

There were two more rounds of competition that day. Evelyn participated in each one. She won the tournament. After the awards assembly was concluded, I found the Baileys and Evelyn standing together.

"I told you Ms. Evelyn should have won, and she did," said our newest lay judge.

"I would like to try the event, but don't know how to find the right play," Sarah declared.

"We have a bunch of cuttings in our library you can examine next week when you officially come and join our speech team," declared Evelyn.

"Oh, she will be there," said Mrs. Bailey.

"Oh, mom, let me talk for myself; even if I am sick on Monday, I will be there and meet all of you who better get ready for another drama diva," she said smiling.

"I think I have the right piece you could use. It is a new choreopoem that I have recently found. I will give it to you to read and then share the cutting that is waiting for someone to perform. It will take some coaching because of all the subtle mountains and valleys of emotion that must be captured. But, in the end if done correctly, should be as powerful as any other piece being performed," I declared to all who wanted to hear. After all, I had given the opportunity to the three black students I felt could have brought it to life, but all had passed.

Although Sarah was only a freshman at the school and was only fourteen years old, she had probably read more than most seniors and had watched comedy and drama on television. She was one of the easiest students I ever had the privilege of coaching. She listened to what I said was needed and then delivered it her way. She won her first competition performing *"For Colored Girls"* with first place marks from every single judge. Comments included from "Overwhelming," "Most powerful piece I have heard," "You should be in senior division!" were written on her evaluation forms.

I took Sarah out of the novice division and put her in the senior division at our next invitational tournament at USC. Evelyn took first place and Sarah took second place. This new drama duo was born. For the remainder of the year, Evelyn and Sarah were the top two finishers for us in dramatic interpretation. Evelyn felt partially responsible for developing Sarah as a solid dramatic interpreter. I loved seeing the admiration the two had for each other.

Evelyn won the national qualifier and Sarah placed second and was the alternate. At the California State Finals, Evelyn placed second and Sarah placed first. She was first place in California as a freshman.

Both students went to nationals. Sarah placed sixth at nationals. Evelyn was a simi-finalist. Evelyn was so appreciative of the fact she had done her best. She was happy with the outcome. She knew she could only control the things she had rehearsed and executed at her highest level. Sarah had risen to such a high ranking in such a short time, she felt the coaching by Evelyn, the other interpreters, and me were a given and would happen each year.

Sarah was determined to be the national champion the next year because of the tutelage that had been given to her by the entire squad. She was actively reading new novels, plays, and poems determined to find the next piece she could use. She even wanted to help coach the new students.

Unfortunately, because I left Bakersfield High School at the end of that academic year, Sarah never qualified to go to the state finals nor nationals for the remainder of her high school competitive career. She was talented enough, but either never found the right cutting, did not have the proper coaching, or a combination of both.

Sarah taught me for the first time in my career, I knew that my talents as a coach were outstanding, and I should stop questioning myself whether I was good enough to coach any event that was found in the world of forensic competition.

CHAPTER FIFTEEN: BAKERSFIELD HIGH SCHOOL

Theodore Smith

t was my third-year teaching at Bakersfield High School, and I felt that it would be the year that all my work, and thousands of hours of rehearsals, and research was about to come to fruition. The only weak point in the array of my speaker strengths was a knockout persuasive speaker.

I had asked some of the students to attend the USC Summer Forensics Workshop where well recognized high school speech coaches provided special one-on-one training within their areas of expertise, and college debaters and college debate coaches offered workshops in debate strategy, debate topic analysis, and specific individual event areas.

If you could afford to attend this workshop your odds of winning at your state level tournaments or the national qualifying tournaments were much stronger. I asked the booster club to raise money so we could send ten of our students to this summer experience. When the booster club failed to raise enough money, I paid the difference.

One of the booster parents came into my office the week before our students were leaving for USC. She was very concerned about her son who was an outstanding academic student, excelled in sports, but did not participate in other outside activities. She felt he could benefit by attending the individual events portion of the USC workshop.

"Mr. Reel, my son is Theodore Smith, and my husband and I have witnessed the transformation of this program here at the school since you took over and want our son to benefit. If we were to pay his way to this workshop at USC, would you be willing to allow him to participate?" she asked.

"Mrs. Smith, it is my understanding that any student can attend the workshop if they enroll and pay the participation fee to USC. Does your son want to participate?" I asked, wanting to find out more about her son and why this mother was trying to broker a place for her son whom I didn't even know wanted to attend, or how he might benefit, or if he would soon be competing for us.

"We feel that once he is forced to participate with other young men and women from your group, he will not only want to participate, but will be quite successful," she said smiling like a good ambassador might do when brokering a deal.

"I only want students who want to rise to the next level to attend this summer. The students we are sending have all worked hard, participated, and made a commitment to become the best speakers possible. I don't know your son. Does he even know you and your husband want him to attend a workshop that will be very demanding and place great expectations on him?" I asked.

"Theodore is the type of young man who will listen to those around him and will see how forensics can benefit his ability to attend college. He feels that football will be his ticket into college, but we fear he might get hurt and then those hopes would go away." she said now sitting down. I could tell she loved her son and wanted him to succeed.

"I would need to talk to him before recommending he attend such a workshop representing our school. If you pay the entire amount for him for the seven days, it would be several hundred dollars." I explained, seeking further clarification as to the commitment level she was providing.

"That is quite acceptable. We both work, and with two completely different types of boys, we can provide any funds that would be needed to benefit anything that either of our sons wants or needs," she said rising to stand next to me.

"When can I meet your son? It would need to be just the two of us. I don't want you to be able to influence anything he says. He needs to decide for himself. I want him to feel able to tell the truth and not be afraid of hurting your expectations he might feel you have about him or the direction he wants for himself." I said as I looked directly into her eyes and started gathering things off my desk.

"I will get him to come and see you today about 4:30 p.m. Is that acceptable?" she asked.

"I am only meeting with him to see if this is something he wants to do!" I shared, reaffirming my position regarding Theodore's wanting this to take place. At exactly 4:30 p.m. the door to my classroom opened and a tall, handsome, athletic looking young man entered.

"Mr. Reel, my parents asked me to visit with you and explain why we feel my attendance at the USC Forensics Summer Workshop would benefit me and the team I would become a part of immediately," he said moving closer to my desk at the front of the class. He looked like an outstanding and outgoing student who seemed well adjusted. He smiled at me. "Well, part of that is true. First, it is an honor to meet with you. You certainly know how to make an entry. Please sit. Do you know anything about forensics?" I asked wanting to get ready for many more questions I would have.

"I know it is about students who give speeches on different topics and compete against other students from their own school as well as other schools for competition, trophies, and some type of recognition that provides those students extra points during the initial application process to major colleges," he said smiling as he sat down in the chair and desk in the front middle section of my classroom.

"With all of this knowledge, you have not wanted to participate before this summer?" I asked.

"My parents were older (in their forties) when they had me. We have planned my education together ever since I have a memory. They have always looked after what was best for me. They want me to do better than what they have done financially and become something I can be proud of as I get older.

I greatly appreciate the time, energy, and money they have spent providing the best tutors, coaches, and even participating in booster clubs, volunteering on school committees, and giving funds to support areas we feel will benefit me," he explained.

"But what about you. What do you want? What are your dreams?" I asked pausing to give him ample time to respond.

"I want the best for me. I do realize that one bad catch and tackle might end my football career we have worked on since I played Pop Warner. As an articulate, semi-good looking, and athletic person, I can start a back-up plan with public speaking," he said laughing and smiling. He appeared very confident for such a young man.

"The students attending this program all have experience, desire, and talent," I responded so he would know it would be challenging. I did not want Theodore to think he would have an advantage.

I wanted him to see the extreme disadvantage he would take into the workshop.

"I have as much talent as anyone once I am told how to express it. My desire is to be the best I can be, and experience is a learned process which I can learn as fast if not faster than anyone else." Theodore responded.

"Have you ever written a speech?" I asked, wanting to know just how much special attention the people at USC would have to provide him.

"I have written many essays so I think I can adapt that knowledge from the written format into the speaking format of delivering what the coaches and I decide is an appropriate topic." he shared thinking he had won the battle.

"It is not quite that easy. There are certain ways to structure arguments, development of main points, and utilization of creative opening introductory attention devices and conclusions that make the audience want to go forth to support the cause you are proclaiming," I responded back as quickly as possible. His answer would tell me much about what he thought important outside of his parents' opinion.

"What do you or the team have to lose? If I don't excel, the coaches there will tell you about my limited skills and whether you should spend time developing me as a speaker. If I perform as I think I will, you, my team, and I all benefit. Don't you think that should be our goal?" he responded to me.

"I am willing to send you if you tell me right now you want to try this and you have thought about it, and you are not being forced to go by your parents." I tried requiring him to take a stance for himself.

"They want me to try it. I want to try it. I am not practicing football nor studying for any of my classes, because I am not in summer school. This would be my summer school for this year. What do you say?" he asked, rising from the desk.

"I will let USC know you are arriving completely as a novice speaker, but they should prepare themselves for seeing an amazing growth in just nine days." I declared. I wanted him to leave feeling I was supporting his monumental endeavor.

When Theodore returned, it was an amazing transformation. He made an appointment with me to share the persuasive speech he had written and performed at the USC Institute. He placed second in the open division. His delivery was impeccable. His presence was in-the-minute causing me to feel his topic was the most important topic that needed attention. I had to spend some time on my own to digest just how powerful that speech and topic might be if he were competing in an open division with senior competitors.

"Theodore, I am impressed and know you can become a very powerful and successful competitor. That speech, just the way it is at this moment in time, can get you to the final round at most tournaments. I am afraid the topic is not quite unique enough for you. Is there anything you can think of that really gets to you about a limitation or discrimination that takes place and makes you really upset?" I asked trying to elicit a topic he felt so strongly about for himself.

I wanted him to come up with a topic that would bring out his real and honest core feelings to expose that topic in his own way.

"I am very concerned about something," Theodore said. He paused and waited to see if I was going to respond.

"Are you going to share it with me?" I asked.

"I am a straight "A" student, starting end on the football team, black, and none of my new teachers expect me to be as bright or brighter than my other classmates. They stereotype me immediately," he shared with sincerity and concern.

"Why don't we work on a speech about stereotyping? I don't think I have heard a competitive speech by a male on that topic. You may have already identified your three main points. Stereotyping in sports, academics, and racially. Keep the speech you created at USC for the beginning of the year, but soon we will have a new speech that will be a message you want to share, and people will want to hear!" I promised.

I spent the next few days trying to create how we might approach this topic. I had asked Theodore to begin researching facts, statistics, and examples regarding stereotyping. I wanted him to get special recognition and wanted any audience member hearing and seeing his speech to stereotype him at the very beginning unconsciously at best. We went out and bought him a very nice three piece pinstriped black and white suit, a black brim hat, and some very shiny black shoes. I also bought an identical three piece pinned striped black and white suit.

When we traveled to invitationals for him to quickly earn a reputation, I wanted those coaches to know he was my student, and when we walked past people dressed the same it certainly worked.

He looked like a model when he stood up to present his topic. He walked to the front during each presentation in a certain predetermined walking cadence and positioned himself with his hands and arms crossed, looking down at his feet, and then as he would step forward, he went and pulled the brim down just a bit more, and then looked straight out to the center of the audience and said,

"Say baby, what's happenin? Theodore Shame is my name, and making love is my game. Fifty bucks will get you one night of sure delight," and would pause and wait for the audience to react and then continue, "While Theodore Shame may be my name, why should making love be my game?" He would proceed to preview the topics of discussion regarding the stereotyping that is done in sports, academics, and in race relationships.

Theodore quickly rose to being one of the most successful persuasive speakers on the competitive circuit. People were coming to the rounds to hear his speech. He would get standing ovations in elimination rounds. He became a true star.

I also paired him with another debater who needed a partner, and they soon became very competitive and were far exceeding my expectations. In local tournaments with lay judges, they were part of our winning teams when we would close out the tournament because we had the top two or four teams and did not have to debate ourselves. This notoriety, however, ended abruptly.

Theodore and his partner were competing in the semi-final round of debate at our state qualifying tournament. They were facing a team from another school who were affirming a similar case to the one they were running. We had done as much research regarding the topic as any other team. We had in our possession all the original source citation documents in case anyone challenged us regarding the information we provided during any round of competition.

We carried the original materials for certain arguments because some teams were deleting or adding words that helped their position. These teams were not being honest in their presentations. We never called it plagiarism, but instead, we called it a mistake in translation. We made sure the judges knew it was a breach of ethics and they were cheaters.

In one of our practices earlier in the week, against our top team, they read a piece of evidence which, had it been true, would have proven the major premise of the argument to be invalid. The evidence was altered or falsified. When our other team confronted them about where they had discovered the evidence and to show them the original documentation, they confided they had made it up to give our top team a heart attack and promised to not use the evidence. They were at a point where they did not want the superior team to win and were willing to try anything.

I asked them to get rid of the evidence and made them promise not to use such evidence because they would lose a round of competition for falsifying evidence, be removed from the tournament, and they would be known as cheaters. I always wanted the students to know how important it is was to tell the truth in a round of debate. Winning arguments with falsified evidence cannot be tolerated.

I wanted them to be known as having integrity and to be known as never participating against time honored truth for a temporary win. Sure enough, in their next competition, they used the evidence in a round against another school. The coach from the other team sought me out and shared with me what had been done. In that round, the other team asked them to see the questionable evidence that had been used. My team refused to allow them to see the evidence. The evidence they used in that round was being challenged by that team and their coach. I went to them, and they confessed what they had done. They were given a loss in that debate, but the other team did not press any charges of plagiarism against them.

I did not allow them to advance in the debate competition.

After the tournament, I shared with them that neither would be attending the state finals. By not being allowed to attend the state tournament, they could not participate in their individual events either. This caused an immediate controversy at the school. The heated exchanges were not comfortable!

Theodore, who many thought would win the state finals was part of a decision to falsify evidence in a debate round. He felt that individual events and debate were two separate parts of competition and did not feel the harsh punishment was justified. What he did not know was I had met with my principal and explained the situation to him about cheating and the prior incident warning that had been given to the two of them.

"There are two different things going on with the behavior exhibited by the two of them. One is disregard of truthfulness of what is right and wrong. The other is lack of respect for self that led to the stooping to a level to win at all costs. We need to set an example so that our students and the students within our league know we won't tolerate unprofessional and unacceptable behavior when representing our school," my principal said during this meeting.

Some of the parents did not want to accept the position the principal took. They took their case to the district superintendent and had the principal summoned to the district office.

Two weeks later, after the district supported both the principal and me, my home became the victim of egg tossing, and water balloons filled with paint hitting the front windows. One night my home was burglarized, and my house contents tossed around, and dishes were broken and left out on the floor or counters.

I cannot tell you how I felt when I arrived home and saw my refuge, my place of solitude. It made me feel violated and even as an adult afraid of what might have happened to me had I been home.

I called the police, but nothing could be proven. One of my neighbors said they remembered seeing an older truck parked down the street. They could not identify the make or model. One of the boys had owned an older truck, but I had no proof Theodore, or his partner were the culprits.

Some of the parent fund raisers went to the principal and asked him to fire me because I had made charges against students that could not be substantiated. They suggested the group might not continue to support the program if action against me were not taken.

The principal called me into his office to discuss my way of doing things. We both knew he was supportive with what I had done.

"I am having this meeting because I promised the booter parents I would meet with you. I told them from my standpoint, you did exactly as I would have done. At that point, the two parents of the two students you disciplined expressed their very much opposition. They even alluded to the point of considering legal action against you. I told them anyone can sue another person, but this school would back your actions." he said.

Even though I knew I would be backed by my principal, I was tired and frustrated with my working tirelessly for what I thought was making a change and giving students a chance to succeed. I felt unappreciated and not respected by certain people. I really felt betrayed by the booster club and some of the parents!

I thought I was making a positive change in the students' lives. I found myself constantly battling with people in the Bakersfield area who wanted to place obstacles in the way of helping their children become positive influences in society. It was a very difficult decision to walk away from the students I loved and knew had so much potential. Part of me wanted to stay for them. I also weighed what I needed. For once, I needed to take care of me more than to continue fighting parents.

When I discussed my plan to leave BHS, my principal informed me the person who was the second runner-up when I was hired still wanted my job. He had already contacted the principal because he had been told by one of the boosters I would not be returning. I felt he would gain much from what I was leaving and would have great talent waiting to be on display. I decided to take a year off and leave education while I sorted out whether forensics was something I wanted to continue doing. I retreated to the bay area and left education. I became a waiter.

Once I resigned as the coach, the chaos associated with my home ceased. Those booster parents thought they had succeeded. One of the two students I had disciplined even stopped by my classroom on my last day to congratulate me on my decision.

"I just wanted to stop by and thank you for resigning from teaching here. It will allow all the students to return next year and continue the dreams each of us have! Had you chosen to continue teaching here you would have experienced some very uncomfortable housing problems, missing papers, and even challenges to your health you thought were private, but maybe leaked out," he warned. What he did not know was I had not run out of town. I chose to leave!

I now knew who was responsible for doing the things to my home. It was not a coincidence that a certain student shared incriminating information on the day he felt relief of responsibility for the things he did. I decided my efforts would be better spent someplace else.

Theodore and his parents taught me to listen to parents who had dreams and aspirations for their children, but to always insist and validate the student wanted the same dream for him/herself. I also learned that some people change support and acceptance of you when they feel their child has been persecuted for no reason.

Most parents do not want to take your word over their child. I learned to document so I could validate any claims.

CHAPTER SIXTEEN: FRESNO CHRISTIAN ACADEMY

Susan Boyle

I had taken a year off from teaching and had moved to Antioch, California. I got a job as a waiter at a restaurant called the *River View Lodge*. It had its own boat dock and air landing strip. I was the first male server they ever hired. There are some great stories to tell about that experience, but it will have to wait for another time.

From Antioch, I moved back to the Fresno area and accepted a job at a private Christian school where I felt I could provide some role modeling and hoped the students would be smarter, be better behaved, and possess more motivation than those I had taught in public schools.

The principal at *Fresno Christian Academy* promised me when she hired me that the school would fund the competition speaking program at whatever level I developed it and would make sure we were able to attend all the tournaments that were needed to gain a good reputation for the school. I was given one period off from teaching to prepare all the logistics for travel, entry, and make accommodations for students and judges needed to support our adventures. I was instructed to ask any and every student I met if they were interested in participating in competition public speaking. My schedule of classes looked like this:

Period One:	9th Grade Grammar
Period Two:	9th Grade Grammar
Period Three:	11th Grade American Literature
Period Four:	11th Grade American Literature
Lunch	
Period Five:	12th Grade Writing
Period Six:	Class Preparation
Period Seven:	Forensics Preparation

For the first two days I simply taught to the best of my ability. I had some parts of each class where I would lecture, a part where students were asked to share, a part where we talked about current events, a part where the students wrote about topics I gave them, and a time when they could ask any questions they felt needed to be addressed. It was my fourth day of teaching at Fresno Christian when I met Susan Boyle. She was a cute, vivacious, and extremely intelligent young woman. We were discussing various American authors when she informed the class, she had performed a cutting from *To Kill a Mockingbird* in her 9th grade class at a different school prior to being sent to this private school and told us her classmates shared it helped them understand what was taking place in the book they were forced to read.

"Susan, what if we were to meet after school today and plan how you might make something like that into a part of competition speech?" I asked.

"That is fine with me. I loved competing in speech when I was at the public school," she said smiling like all the students knew what she was discussing with me.

"You participated in forensics before?" I asked.

"Yes, I participated during my first freshman year in public school. I wasn't a good student then and when I transferred here, I had to repeat my freshman year because of all the bad grades I had earned," she said smiling and waiting for a response from me. Her statement about not being a good student seemed to shock the class. Some of the students made comments.

"If you were getting bad grades, I cannot imagine what my parents would have done to me," said Simon.

"Tell me your secret to becoming so brainy so I can jump on that band wagon," called out Olivia.

"She is the next smartest person here next to Darla," called out James.

"Ok, we need to get back on track. We cannot change the past, only today and hopefully the future!" I said moving directly to the front of the classroom.

I waited for the day to end so I could talk privately with Susan. She arrived, but she also brought Darla with her. I did not question whether she felt she needed an escort, or they were simply good friends.

"Please come in and let's talk. Both of you have a seat. Susan, did you use your cutting from *To Kill a Mockingbird* in competition?" I asked.

"No. I had been using another piece that was very well received. I won some competitions with very little coaching. I think I would like my old cutting of *To Kill a Mockingbird* and see about doing it in competition," she said pausing to see my response.

"You never used any material from *To Kill a Mockingbird* in competition and you have not competed since that time?" I responded with a question I hoped would be the answer that would be positive for both of us.

"Nope. We have never had a speech program here since I arrived. Do you think we could get me involved again? It will be nice to see if my old coach is still coaching. The only thing she really did was just take us to tournaments. I think you will do more that drive us." she said smiling.

"You don't have to worry about not being coached. I will hear you a million times if necessary. I want every aspect of the cutting you do to be perfected. Go get the book and read it from cover to cover. I will do a cutting for you, and you do a cutting, and we will partnership and combine the best of both cuttings. How does that sound?" I asked, turning my head to include Darla, and finding out why she was accompanying Susan.

"Darla, are you here as a bodyguard for Susan, or are you interested in becoming part of what will become a very successful speech team? Some might even call it the new dynasty!" I responded to Susan's friend.

"I wanted to see what you are like outside of class and to seek clarification for each of the events. Would it be possible to review some of the literature you have regarding each of the events and the rules and regulations for those events?" she asked as though she were doing research for a doctoral thesis. I could already tell Darla was one of the brightest students I had met.

"I just happen to have created a flyer with such material for outstanding students like you. Let me go to my desk and retrieve tonight's reading after you have completed your homework." I joked with her. I knew she would have it memorized by the next time we saw each other.

Susan took about a week to read the book and provide me with her cutting of what she wanted to perform. It was interesting that our cuttings were very similar and we in collaboration tweaked it so slightly. The cutting was exceptional. It was not the version most people had performed. One of the most unique aspects was a female was going to perform it instead of a male. The years of voice training for Susan paid off because she could perform two distinct male voices with such authenticity most high school boys could not muster those deep resonant sounds.

She won every local tournament we attended that year. Right before the state qualifier, we attended the San Luis Obispo Invitational. She was quite a buzz at the tournament. Coaches and students were telling each other they needed to go and watch this amazing competitor. Susan grew quite the cult following at each tournament she attended.

When the semi-final round of dramatic interpretation was posted, Susan was sixth speaker in panel one. The room was so full of onlookers there was not a single seat left. In fact, some were sitting on the floor. Susan did a masterful performance. She received a standing ovation from the entire audience including her fellow competitors at the end of her program. We all knew she would be in the final round.

However, when the final round was posted

Susan was not one of the finalists. I was not the only one confused. Many of the students and coaches who had watched her in the semi-final round wanted to know what happened. One of the judges came up to me personally and asked me to challenge the staff. He felt some error had taken place. The tournament had what is called a closed tabulation room.

No person not working as tournament staff could go into the room. I personally did go and ask to talk with the tournament director. I knocked on the door. The person that came to the door was a student from the college and was one of their top debaters.

"Hello, is Dr. Eddinger available? I feel a mistake may have taken place in the dramatic interpretation category." I questioned the young man.

"He has run home but will be back soon. I can assure you no mistake has taken place. We double checked all the scores. Sometimes students feel they have done better than what took place." he said, starting to close the door.

"Is it possible for me to see the scores for my student, she has won every tournament this year and I want to verify the outcome especially since Dr. Eddinger is not on campus." I questioned the student who was doing his best considering the situation.

"If we let you, then we would have to let all the other coaches who think their student should have made the finals of any of the events. You will get her evaluations at the end of the tournament, and they will verify no mistake was made." he responded and immediately closed the door.

I certainly did not want to make a scene. I knew Dr. Eddinger and respected him as a coach and tournament director. I went back and tried to explain to our team what I was told and that we would see the results at the end of the tournament on our way home.

Once the tournament ended and I picked up the results for all the students, each of our members wanted to sort out the evaluation cards and get to the bottom of the confusion. I asked them to wait until we were in the van driving home. I wanted us to be removed from the college to give us privacy and time to heal if needed and to protect the tournament staff in case there was a problem. As we were driving out of the parking lot, I handed the results to Darla and asked her to distribute them to each competitor. She began calling out names and events so students could read the comments and placements for each round of competition for each event. Susan assembled her comments and began reading the results aloud.

"Round One 1st: Round Two 1st : Round Three

1st : Semi-Finals: 1st 1st 1st ." She certainly should have advanced to the finals. I quickly asked them to read the tournament spreadsheet for her event. Somehow, the scores for her Semi-final round had been recorded as 4th, 4th, 4th. A tab person had not recorded her scores properly. The students wanted me to turn the van around and go back and demand the tournament staff apologize and give her the first-place trophy. Once we arrived home, I called Dr. Eddinger who profusely apologized and sent Susan a very large 1st place trophy in the mail. I was glad he lived up to his mistake, but that mistake did not help her reputation as being the only undefeated dramatic interpreter in the state because all of those attending that invitational did not know a mistake had been made.

Susan went to the state qualifying tournament held at one of the local high schools as a major contender for the championship that would allow her to attend the state tournament. Susan did take first place and was spectacular as usual.

After the tournament, my friend, Don Vettel, well respected coach in the Bakersfield area, shared with me that some of the coaches were discussing ways they might prevent Susan from attending the state tournament. A couple of Fresno coaches and her previous coach felt because she had competed her original freshman year when she was in public school, her eligibility started that year whether she had competed during the next three years of her high school career. They decided that since she had retaken her freshman year, she was a 5th year senior and was ineligible to compete.

Within a week, we received an official letter from the California State Tournament staff making such allegations. The actual coach who was making such allegations had a student who was a 5th year student but had only participated in forensics during his last four years. His 5 years of sports did not make him ineligible because that had nothing to do with speech competition.

I went to the principal, Mrs. Hansen, and then we both went to the senior pastor who was responsible for the finances for the school. I asked him to hire an attorney to fight these allegations. He listened and met with the attorney the church and school used. That attorney informed him the cost might be forty thousand dollars or so to fight the charges. The school chose not to represent Susan nor our program. Susan and the team were devastated. I tried to find a way to finance such an undertaking myself. Unfortunately, I was not able to get the funds needed. I could not get any attorney to take the case on retainer or pro bono.

Susan did not go to the state or nationals. She lost her desire to compete and after graduation did not pursue forensics in college. I feel she would have won many more titles if the competition would not have been so political.

A few very mean men burst the hopes and aspirations of a young lady who had finally learned to accept herself and found her inner joy. Susan taught me to fight such academic bullies who stand in the way of what is right, so they benefit instead of students. All three of those coaches were near the end of their academic lives, and soon voluntarily retired or were forced to do so. I learned that when such people leave, our activity becomes better. Susan taught me there is no place in any form of competition where the coaches should subvert the outcome of true student success to benefit their own students!

CHAPTER SEVENTEEN: FRESNO CHRISTIAN ACADEMY

Darla Mathews

One afternoon when we were working on Susan's dramatic interpretation, I noticed another girl just hanging around the door; she would not come into the room, but she also did not want to get so far from the door she could not see what we were doing. I noticed when Susan left the room this other girl headed down the staircase with her. The two looked as though they were the best of friends. Both were laughing and pushing and teasing each other. I thought I recognized the other person but was not sure. Her hair was down and covered most of her face. She was slightly shorter than Susan, but I noticed her shoes were hanging over her shoulder. That would account for some of the height differences.

The next session with Susan, I noticed the same person hanging out in the hallway.

"Susan, do you think your friend would like to come in and sit down while we practice?" I asked.

"Oh, no I am sure she is fine. Her dad is a pretty famous doctor in town, and she does not get along with her stepmom. So, she spends as much time here at school as she can, so she doesn't have to go home early each day," she said progressing to the front of the classroom preparing to do another run-through of her presentation.

"She looks familiar, but I am not sure of her name." I said, trying to get Susan to share with me the name of the girl lurking in the hallway.

"She is in one of your classes. I thought you knew each of your students," Susan said, as she positioned herself to begin the presentation.

"I don't know anyone who looks like her," I said, now very confused with what was taking place.

"She always wears her hair up and she never is seen during regular hours with her make-up, designer clothes, and her bright pink ink pen, Susan said quickly and slightly less loud than if she were starting her performance.

"That is not Carla. She is much taller and is always posed as a model. This girl looks unkept and is much shorter." I said, waiting to see if Susan was going to perform or talk about her friend.

"Let me prove it to you. Carla, come in here and talk with Mr. Reel." she said.

"He doesn't believe it is you, get your butt in here now," she ordered, motioning for her friend to come inside the classroom. The young woman came to the middle of the doorway but did not enter the room.

"Hi, it's me. I never get a chance to hang out with my friends because my stepmom doesn't like any of them and is afraid, they will corrupt me and I won't get into one of the prestigious colleges they have decided I should attend," she contended while all this information came out without any coaxing from either of us.

"I am so sorry I did not recognize you. You are always welcome in my classroom. If you sit here long enough perhaps you will decide to participate. I am sure your parents will be impressed because forensics is considered as a very high-level extracurricular activity for consideration to many screeners in the college community." I said searching for a way Carla could fit into our level of acceptance.

"It's OK. I dress down so not many people know who and where I go prior to me being forced to go back to the penitentiary each night." she said quickly and succinctly.

"I don't think it is that bad," I said smiling and hoping for the best.

"Yes, it is!" both girls said in unison.

"Is that a little exaggeration?" I asked.

"You don't know how much of a witch her stepmom can be. She is just evil and really hates Carla but loves Carla's brother Jimmy who is in the seventh grade here at Fresno Christian." confided Susan.

"Carla, why don't you talk with your father about how you feel?" I asked, hoping she would say he was a good person and felt loved enough to discuss her issues with him.

"She doesn't do it around him. She portrays herself as *Mrs. Cleaver* until he leaves the room. She then blinks her eyes, puckers her lips, sticks out her tongue, or whispers the words, 'He loves me, and you can't do anything about it.' But guess what? I can! I can do what I want. I don't have to be perfect, never raising my voice, always getting straight "A's" because that is what is expected." she said, now becoming very emotional.

"You are one of the brightest students at this school. You do get "A's" in every one of your classes.

Every teacher talks about you and Darla Owens. "Darla's mother supports and loves her. Unfortunately, my mother died, and this replacement finds me threatening and that hurts me because I just want a mother to love me also!" Carla claimed. She realized she was crying and sat down.

"How about trying something that will occupy much of your free time and will help you get into the college you want. Your stepmom won't be able to not let you participate because we will have you join Darla who wants a debate partner who is as bright as she is and can learn things quickly. The two of you will be prize examples of two very smart but very different styles that will make a stand for young women in debate as opposed to only having boys be the main stars. Does that sound like a challenge you might be willing to take?" I asked.

"I would have to think about it. Darla is so smart, and I don't know if I can learn as quickly or be as good as I know she can become." Carla said, trying her best to find a way out.

"Darla and I are searching for a partner that can be as committed as she will become. You are trying not to go home early and want to be something that your stepmom did not decide for you to become. Sounds like the two of you need each other," I said, in the best counseling voice I could muster.

"I don't like to play sports because all the various ones cause you to sweat. How much learning do we need to do before we start winning?" Carla asked, making me think she was moving in the right direction for our team. Darla had told me she was ready to start to become the best she could!

"I can have the two of you ready to start in Novice division in about three weeks. You should be in the final round of your first tournament if you start now and practice as hard as I know Darla will," I claimed proudly.

"Do you think we should have a meeting with

Darla and see if she agrees, see if she wants to debate with me? I don't know how we will get along." Carla said, knowing that Darla was one of the most loved students on campus.

"I will talk with Darla tomorrow right after American Literature. I know she is going to be as happy as I am to call you her debate partner. You are smarter than any other person and that is key to what we must accomplish. Let's meet right after school. You can come as Carla the 'A' student or Carla 'Girl of Intrigue' student."

CHAPTER EIGHTEEN:
FRESNO CHRISTIAN ACADEMY

Darla Owens

From the first-class meeting of my American Literature class, Darla Owens stood out as a bright light and eager student who wanted to do all in her power to be the perfect student. She was well liked by the other students, almost idolized because she was so gracious, kind, and understanding of those who had not been given the academic prowess she had been provided by God. She was quick to make sure she was inclusive in each of her classroom discussions by often asking other students to provide their point of view while not dominating the discussion but helping me guide the discussion in a productive and entertaining fashion. She was like having an outstanding teaching assistant!

I soon found out from other faculty members that Darla was not only as smart as she appeared, but many of my colleagues felt she was perhaps the smartest student they had ever taught. Two of the teachers told me she had a photographic memory. She was the one student who had received the highest-class grade from every single teacher in every single class she had taken. From the first week at Fresno Christian Academy, I felt Darla would find the way to become part of a national honor elite team of those few that would tell others later in life she was a national champion in high school forensics. I just had to find the right venue for her to dominate and conquer.

I had the students reading *The Scarlet Letter* for the first of four books that were mandatory. I had suggested to these very wealthy and savvy students that this was a novel about a great love story that was told many years ago and found themselves in situations that we could now discuss in public. A couple of the boys suddenly wanted to read their first novel.

I was lecturing one day about one specific item that was to take place in the reading assigned for that evening. Darla raised her hand and said when called upon:

"Mr. Reel, I think that actually took place in last night's reading if my fellow classmates had done their reading."

"I might be off, but my lecture notes indicate it takes place in tonight's reading," I said.

"If you want to turn to page 137 of the novel, I think you will find it. I am not trying to prove you wrong, because your lectures are always so entertaining and full of excitement, but I think I remember reading it last night," she said waiting for my answer.

"You may be correct Darla, but I don't think it really matters when it was read, but the fact the information given in the reading is outlined in my notes and lecture," I said, now waiting for her answer.

"I was just trying to make your lecture more accurate," she said. One of the students sitting behind her; a boy, whispered loudly enough for most of the class to hear,

"Don't mess with her, she is always correct!" Many of the other students either shook their heads in agreement, had something to say aloud that was supportive, or simply smiled and waited for class to resume. For the remainder of the class, I was on my best lecture etiquette so I would not be challenged again by a seventeen-year-old.

Darla had as close to one-hundred-percent recall as I had ever seen. She loved devouring magazine articles, books, and textbooks. I felt she could compete almost immediately in impromptu speaking and extemporaneous speaking categories because of her innate knowledge. I asked her to see me after school so I could explain the difference between the two events. She agreed to meet with me, and I found myself in not only an intellectual discussion, but a very stimulating discussion about current events.

"The basic difference between the two is that extemporaneous speaking utilizes and requires source citations within the body of the speech from the major magazines that are weekly, monthly, and quarterly. They include *Time, Newsweek, US* and *News Report,* monthly and or quarterly magazines like *Mother Jones, the American Medical Association Journal,* and major newspapers like the *NY Times,* LA *Times,* and the *Fresno Bee.*" I said waiting for her to correct my last statement.

"Do you really think the *Fresno Bee* is a major publication?" she asked. I had her fall into my trap.

"I was just wanting to make sure you were listening to me!" I replied.

"I always listen to you. I don't always agree with you, but I feel you are older and as an elder, I will always respect and give you the benefit of the doubt in telling the truth you know it because of your age," she said, now smiling and waiting for me to respond.

"It is nice of you, a young teenage girl, to respect your elders," I said now smiling back.

"I am very mature compared to the rest of the girls at this school. I know what I want to do with my life. I am much more mature and could easily enter college and excel at a moment's notice. My younger brother needs me, however, and I try to support him as well as the boys he calls friends. He does not feel that preparing for college should occupy too much time while in high school. He will eventually find out he should have been better prepared." she said now waiting to see if I wanted to further the conversation.

"What makes you so prepared?" I asked to try to find out more insightful information from Darla.

"It is a combination of what my parents taught me, what they provided to me as learning opportunities, my faith in God, and my devotion to being responsible and sharing such with both my male and female friends," she said casually.

"Now, back to the differences between the two events. Impromptu speaking is more general in nature and does not require any source citations because the topics are either one word abstract, a quotation, or general knowledge type questions. It is designed to test your ability to address topics as if they were to come up in everyday conversation. You always get to interpret the topic in a manner you decide to make a thesis statement. I always suggest one spends the two minutes of preparation time prior to delivering the speech in the following formula division: First ask yourself what you think you want to address as your main point of discussion. Make that point the ultimate persuasive point of discussion. Divide the speech into two to three main points that will help you arrive at that point by the end of your speech so you may use those as previews of what is going to be discussed, and then finally spend the last thirty seconds developing an introduction that will creatively gain the attention of the audience, demonstrate your concern for speaking on the topic, preview your main points you want to discuss, and then will allow you to revisit those points at the conclusion of your speech. The first time in the introduction you use future tense of where you are going in the speech; and in the conclusion you use past tense as to where you have been. Seems simple to me. What do you think?" I asked the smartest student I thought existed in the central valley of California.

"I think I understand and can implement such a rudimentary outline format for developing a generic approach to speaking outline formatting. I think we might want to teach such a format to the other students who want to participate in impromptu speaking so they can learn to become effective speakers. If you don't mind, I would like to use the rudimentary approach, but will adapt the format based on the one word, quotation, or knowledge of the topic I possess. How does that sound to you?" she asked me as she paused and smiled to let me know she completely understood.

Darla helped me refine that generic outlining format for our impromptu speakers. It was interesting that sometimes we would have three or four of the final six or seven final round speakers at tournaments and they all had very similar formats for addressing the topic they chose to discuss. None of them used the same exact wording and all were special in their own approach, but that format never let the student down in quickly and effectively organize their topic with specificity and direction that judges appreciated.

I paired Darla and Carla together as a debate team. Neither were sure they wanted to spend the time and energy it would take to become successful within about six months of learning debate. I knew both capable of such an undertaking if I could convince them to use their talents in such a male dominated activity. I wanted them to become the new talked about team not only because they were female, but because they were so much better than the males who were simply repeating arguments and reading evidence they had been provided by their coaches. These two girls were smart, analytical, and could think on their feet. We worked on presentation skills. Many females, because of their higher voices, would raise their volume and at times would sound like they were screaming and had lost control of the argument. Once I shared that phenomenon with them and convinced them not to raise their level of projection and to not match the number of arguments being advanced; but instead, to group arguments that needed to be discussed, and to point out why they were not addressing arguments that did not matter, they quickly started winning most of their rounds.

We were at an invitational at Claremont College, and I had entered them in the senior division even though it was their first semester of competition.

After each round, I would meet with them to ask how the last round had gone and to encourage them to approach the next round as a test to learn, explore, and conquer the opponent; but always in a calm, relaxing, and more intellectual way that screaming at the judge and opposing team. I was standing saying goodbye and wishing them the best of luck in their final round. I had checked and they were hitting a team from West Beverly Hills High School. I knew that meant they were doing well in the competition because that school always had almost all their teams advance into the elimination rounds at every tournament. One of the assistant coaches from that school standing next to the posting turned and as he moved from the posting area approached the coach from Claremont and said,

"We must be horrible today because we are hitting an all-girl team from a Christian school in the Fresno area. I had a feeling we were not doing a good job, and this confirms it," he said upset with his team not knowing the truth about how well either team was doing. The Claremont coach looked at me and responded quickly:

"I think that is one of Ron Reel's teams, and I have never seen one of his teams not be prepared. You might be surprised just how good the team is even if you don't know them yet!" The assistant coach looked back and simply gave a nonverbal hand gesture that was not becoming. When the girls met the same team in the final round, he had a different opinion of them. When his team lost to the girls in the final round, he had a different opinion about female debate teams and what they can and cannot do better than male teams.

By the time we got to the state finals Darla confided to me that she was concerned about a young woman from Fresno Herndon High School who in extemporaneous speaking did not tell the truth concerning the sources she used and none of the judges understood or did not know what was taking place.

"What are you saying? Is this student just making up quotations that don't exist?" I asked.

"Well, she tells me that if it helps her point and it is something a particular person might say, she simply assigns a source citation to a made-up quote, tells what she thinks the person would say, and moves on to her next point. So, yes, she fabricates where the information might be found, but because of knowing the stance of the person who is being "quoted" she feels it is plausible for that person to make that statement. She calls it "a white lie," Darla said, complaining for the first time during the entire year.

"What would you like me to do? The two of you are nearly always first and second. Shall we make a charge of making up quotations against her or would you like for me to talk with her coach, or shall we break her leg?" I asked, trying to lift her spirit while letting her know I was also concerned.

"It is always something they might say, but it is not from the source she cites. That is what bothers me the most. She just makes up a source. She doesn't spend her thirty minutes looking throughout her magazines. Her coach jokes about it with her, they call her, 'The Estimator' because she estimates what she says is close enough. The rest of us are forced to arrange where the sources come from and check to make sure we are using the correct magazines or other sources; that is all I have to say!" she said now completely worn out and finally able to express frustration with another person.

"Darla, you don't really have to use that time going through the file with your memory, do you?" I asked.

"I don't have to, but I verify just to make sure I am 100% sure where I read the information. I don't like when none of the judge's challenge when she says certain information has come from that *U.S.* and *World Report* article that would never take that stance because it does not report on that kind of topic. Don't these judges read the articles also?" Darla asked, knowing for sure some of the judges were just parents who never read any of the magazine articles.

Darla and that other student continued to be the top two extemporaneous speakers in California. One won the national qualifying tournament and the other the state finals allowing both to qualify for the nationals in their public speaking events. Both advanced into the elimination rounds in extemporaneous speaking. Neither went to the final round.

Darla took first place in the nation in Impromptu Speaking.

Darla and Carla did not qualify for nationals in debate. It was still too early for such a gender breakthrough! I learned that young women are just as capable and sometimes more willing to be coached in debate than boys. Today's statistics from the National

Forensics Association point out that in high school debate girls compose 56 percent of participants with boys responsible for 42 percent. Some participants did not delineate a gender preference.

Unfortunately, I lost contact with Carla, and have not had any communication about where she is today. I have been able to keep track of Darla's professional achievements. Darla became a successful family therapist-counselor. She has always given to others and many people enhanced their well-being and the strength of their family because of her caring and professional guidance.

CHAPTER NINETEEN: FRESNO CHRISTIAN ACADEMY

Stephen Mindle

I had heard about a student attending the school whose parents were one of the wealthiest families in Fresno. He was sixteen, a sophomore, and drove Errol Flynn's 1936 Rolls-Royce to school and parked it in the student parking lot. One would think that would be abnormal for such vintage or expensive cars to be driven by the students attending Fresno Christian Academy. It was not. Over ninety percent of the students attending the school were from families who included either doctors or attorneys. Their parking lot looked like a high-end car-show each day. This stood in direct contrast to the faculty parking lot which housed modest price cars that were almost all four or more years older.

Up to that day, I had never met this student, but the head counselor and the Spanish teacher had shared stories about him. Both suggested he was one of the most caring and helpful students on campus. They warned, however, that he was always seeking attention and did not always make the best choices when it came to acceptable behavior. First period was always just a bit shorter because announcements regarding various activities on campus were presented by our principal, Mrs. Hansen, or by the main attendance secretary, Miss Donovan, each morning at exactly 8:35 a.m. Usually Miss Donovan could be heard throughout the building over the intercom.

"Good morning boys and girls, today's activities have all been cancelled and we are going to be closing the school at noon so the faculty can meet and evaluate the curriculum that some say is too difficult, while others think it is not challenging enough. Stay tuned for further instructions once Pastor Spencer returns from his usual breakfast meeting off campus with any special details," she announced. Some of the students appeared to be unhappy, while others shouted with joy. I tried to calm my class. Just as I had them settled and ready to start class, another announcement began.

"Good morning, this is the real Miss Donovan, and the first announcement was not made by me and if anyone knows who it was, please call the office immediately. There are no announcements today. I repeat, today's activities have not been cancelled, and the school will remain open as usual. Again, if you know who made that announcement, please call the office."

Suddenly students were asking questions.

"Mr. Reel, if it wasn't Miss Donovan on the intercom who do you think it was? It sure sounded like her voice," said Marianne.

"I think they are just messing with us and trying to get us to spill the beans on certain people who they don't like," said Benjamin. He was our conspiracy advocate.

"Class, settle down. We don't know anything at this time, but I am sure we will find out more later today. Let's get back to class," I requested.

During the morning classes I wondered who had been able to sneak into the office, make that announcement, and avoid being seen by anyone. I was also amazed that the person sounded just like Miss Donovan. I wondered whether Miss Donovan had experienced a head injury and shared with all the school what she thought about what should take place at school that day. I quickly dismissed that statement because I did not want to be thought of as participating in conspiracy.

At lunch, a few faculty members were eating and discussing similar situations that had taken place previously. Mr. Sharp, the government teacher, who was known to show many movies during his classes instead of lecturing had experienced a very peculiar movie encounter. Several weeks earlier, as he put that day's video into his projector system, a trailer previewing what was about to be shown appeared that sounded like him, but he had never seen it before. It welcomed the class to "Movies 101" a class designed to modernize the art of lecture by allowing movies to not only supplement but replace the archaic mode of transferring information to students. Sharp never found the person who had engineered that "Special" with narration that sounded just like himself. Mrs. Hernandez, the Spanish teacher, who was teaching for her first time in America, felt like the God of Anger had visited her classroom. She swore it sounded just like Miss Donovan, but it had happened three times since classes had started. She told of what she called the "Intercom Experience" that instructed her to separate her class into various segregated sections of students. Girls were supposed to be seated in the back. While boys towards the front, and any other nationalities were to be seated in seats two or three in any row so she could keep an eye on them to keep them from cheating. Again, Miss Donovan's voice had been used and it had come to her room from the intercom.

By the end of the day, a select committee including the principal, Mrs. Hansen, the assistant principal, Mr. Nelson, the guidance counselor, Mrs. Georgia, and I were requested to investigate the situation. Two anonymous students (they were known to the committee) told us about the person behind all the incidents was Stephen Mindle. Mrs. Hansen summoned Stephen to her office to face our interrogation.

When he arrived, I noticed he was dressed very impressively with matching colors, complementary shirt, pants, shoes, and a sweater that looked like they came from an exclusive clothing store. He had a very contagious smile and was either a very light blonde or a slightly faded redhead.

"Mr. Mindle, it appears according to reliable sources, you have been participating in some shenanigans at this school. Would you like to confess now with a lighter sentence, or do you want us to have a full investigation resulting in a much stiffer result that may lead to expulsion?" she asked. Stephen just looked at each of us and smiled as big as possible.

"I don't know what you are suggesting. I can unequivocally state to each of you, 'I have done no wrong,'" he said, sitting down in the interrogation seat that had been provided for him.

"Mr. Mindle, this is not our first encounter. I had your parents in here on several occasions," stated Mrs. Hansen, being as stern as she could possibly be with such a charismatic person sitting before us.

"You have indeed. I have learned from my mistakes, and you have taught me well. You were gracious last time, and I have taken steps to make sure I personally do nothing wrong here at the school. I do want to remind all of you who don't know that my parents are one of the wealthiest contributors to this school. They have warned me what might happen to the school, and to me, if for any reason they are forced to pull their financial support from Fresno Christian Academy. I would be forced to go to a public school and mixed with some not so acceptable seasoned riftraft lower class beings. I want to remain here where more of my kind of social beings exist," he said, in a mixed statement that sent two various and distinct messages. One was concerning the contributions the school needed to stay in business, and the other to signal that many of the students were there to prevent being sent or bussed to other schools in less wealthy areas of town.

"Mr. Mindle, let me ask you directly the following question, are you responsible for the announcement this morning that sounded like Miss Donovan?"

"Do you really think I could sound like her? I have such a baritone quality to my voice. I don't think I have such a range. Some of the other students who hide their identities might want to cause chaos and disruption. I like reason and tranquility. I think I know who may have made that announcement, but I cannot be sure, and I would be making an unproven accusation that might harm someone because of the lack of proof; and Mrs. Hansen, you have taught me not to participate in inuendo and accusation. May I go now as I have responded to your investigation. I don't think we are any closer to finding the truth than when I arrived," he said, standing to leave.

"Thank you, Mr. Mindle, for coming and being so forthright. I hope what you have said is one hundred percent truthful. Just so we both know, I will always keep my eyes open and watch you every single day," she said, as Stephen left the room. Once he departed the room, she spoke to us.

"Well, I think he was responsible, but no one knows for sure. Keep your eyes and ears open for any further news or reports regarding this incident and any other strange occurrences," she shared, standing up to signal the meeting had been adjourned.

"What makes you think it was him? If he can sound like Donovan, he should go straight to Hollywood," I said, trying to bring some humor to this meeting.

"I have heard him reading stories to the 6th graders from the Muppets, and he has mastered every one of those characters' voices. I don't put it past him to mimic anyone of us!" she concluded. I had not met Stephen before but suddenly I wanted to find a reason to meet him and get him to participate in both speech and drama and find a way to ask him to audition for the musical I had promised to direct for the academic year.

Only two days after this encounter, Stephen stopped by my room to see me. He had a younger girl with him.

"Mr. Reel, I wanted to stop and ask a favor of you. By the way, this is my younger sister, Madelyn," he said motioning for his sister to sit down.

"Well, it is a pleasure to officially meet you. I will do my best to do a favor for you and in turn I will ask you to reciprocate one for me. What is it I do for you?" I asked, moving from the side of the room where I was just finishing a bulletin board about a trip to New York in December. I would be supervising students to see four Broadway shows in five days. I plugged in the lights that flashed to bring extra attention to the board. I needed ten students to make the trip happen and to allow me to have my expenses paid for by the sponsoring company.

"I don't like my English teacher and he does not like me. I want to transfer to your section. I have heard you are much more likeable," he said.

"Do you really think likeability is a reason for changing? What if you decide you don't like me, or God forbid, I decide I don't like you and then it would be impossible for me to transfer you out because there are only two sections this semester of American literature," I said smiling and motioning for him to sit.

"It is more than like. He doesn't get me. He never smiles at my jokes. He is always grumpy. His lectures are boring, and when I must get close to him, he stinks; his breath is so bad I almost puke. Can you find it in your heart to have mercy on me. I will not cause any problems and you will barely know I am a student in your class," he offered his case for my consideration.

"What if my lectures are boring? What if you don't like how I smell? How do we get you through the semester?" I asked in my most sarcastic voice possible.

"I hear from Darla Owens, the smartest girl in this school, your lectures are the best in the entire school. She would never lie. I can tell from here your hygiene is superior and I think you are wearing Polo cologne. It is my favorite. Please!" he insisted.

"I won't transfer you into my section with any of the reasons you have mentioned. I will consider the transfer and will go to your current teacher and ask permission to transfer you because we are going to use some of the work from my class as a way for you to begin participating in my competitive speech program by putting you in Program Reading. This will require you to use a manuscript that we just happen to be examining in my class. It would help me out if I had you in my class each day. How does that sound?"

"If you are willing to do that, I will not let you down and even be your first student to sign up to go to New York in December. I was reading your bulletin board while you were speaking. You will have to come and convince my parents I need to see such professionals to enhance my characters I am performing in whatever event you decide is best for me."

"Stephen, I don't know if you can do various voices. I have heard you can mimic the voice of Miss Piggy. Can you?" I asked.

"Not only her, but I can also imitate the voices of all those characters and many more. Let's form a partnership. You look after me, and I will look after you. What do you say?"

"How do you propose we make this official? You transfer into my English section, and I have your word that you will participate in my speech program. Is that correct?"

"I have heard you are going to cast a musical this semester. I promise I will be one of your stars if you like. That will give more reasons why I will need to see some Broadway shows. Don't forget you will need me to go to New York with you," Stephen quickly responded.

"Do you think I will need a chaperone to travel with me to New York?" I asked smiling as broadly as possible.

"Look, you are going to get a thespian and a forensics student. You are getting a two for one star," he boasted.

I went to Mr. Hanley's room and asked:

"What will it take to have Stephen Mindle transferred into my English section?' I expected some type of negotiations to take place. I was shocked at his quick response.

"How soon can that take place. The sooner the better for me. How is tomorrow? He loves attention and will do anything to get noticed. Let's fill out the paperwork now and he can start in your section tomorrow. There is a God!" he said, as he went to his desk, opened the top drawer, and pulled out a section transfer that only needed a date added. It already had his signature.

Mr. Hanley was right about Stephen needing attention, but I learned that his entire life he had been fighting to gain positive reinforcement from his parents because he could never live up to his older brother who, in their eyes, was flawless in all ways. His brother was completing a four-year college degree at San Diego State. He had been attending the college for six years, but he had convinced his parents that classes were so impacted he could only take two or three classes per semester.

I started giving positive reinforcement to Stephen for his accomplishments and suddenly he would do all I requested of him. Stephen kept his word and auditioned and secured one the major male roles in our musical. Not only did he master his role, but memorized the role I was playing also. He called himself, my understudy. The play was so successfully received, we took it on tour the next semester traveling to three states in two weeks.

In November, I was making the final pitches for the last students who wanted to attend the New York trip. Stephen had been asking me to personally go to his house and ask permission for him to attend. I finally gave in and told him I would meet with his parents.

"Mr. Reel, I know once my parents meet you and you share with them the values and advantages of seeing such professional and high-quality acting that cannot be found in Fresno, they will give me permission to attend. Can you come on Wednesday night at about 5:30 p.m. because both of my parents will have had a martini or two and will be in a better mood. You must make a professional presentation. Wear one of your newer suits. My parents are a bit snobbish. So, let me know the exact time and I will meet you a block away from my house. How is that?" he asked.

"Why are we meeting a block away? Do you not have a driveway?" I countered.

"You will be driving your yellow Nova into the most exclusive neighborhood in Fresno. I don't look down on you, but they might. Let's just keep that from possibly happening."

"I am not ashamed of my car, and if it cannot come into your neighborhood than I can't either." I said firmly.

"I didn't mean any disrespect; I know how little you are being paid here. If you insist on driving to the house, let's make it 7:30 p.m. because it will be dark, and they will have had a few more drinks and won't go out to greet you."

I did go and met both of his parents. They were sitting in their very large family room. Finally, they consented to him going. They wanted to know how much extra money he would need. When I suggested a couple hundred dollars, they insisted he take at least one thousand dollars for incidentals.

We returned from New York and Stephen was confident, excited, and told anyone willing to listen that he had been tutored by the best professional actors working in America. On Monday when school resumed Stephen arrived at my classroom before school started.

"Mr. Reel, I watched how each of those actors made their entry, how they positioned their body when delivering their lines, and where they looked when conveying the message at hand. I paid attention to their facial expressions, and most importantly how each one looked directly at me, and I was moved to laugh, cry, hate, or love their character," he said sitting down waiting to see how I would respond.

"Stephen, did you read some journal article on how an audience member was supposed to feel when experiencing a Broadway show?" I asked, wanting him to share more about what he had read.

"No, you know I don't have time to read those kinds of articles because of all the practice sessions I have been doing on my own program using each of the actors from Broadway as my tutors and inspiration," he claimed.

"Did you sneak backstage and have a conversation with any of the stars we saw?" I now asked, wondering where he had found his information. He appeared to be a different student. He was not joking around, but instead seemed to have changed.

"I did not have to sneak backstage. The two matinee performances when we stayed afterward and the stars came out and talked about why they became hooked on acting, how they had learned from others, and especially what techniques they used to get into the minute for their presentations made me realize that acting is something I want to do and I had the best of the best tell me I can do it," he proclaimed.

Stephen was a natural with voices. His downfall, if I had to find one, was his character placement. We had been working on where to place eye contact for each character and then how to move from placing that character and then returning to establishing direct eye contact with his audience. His placement was usually either too high or low, too one side or the other.

"May I perform my old selection with a new staging developed over the break channeled by several of the Broadway actors you allowed me to visit with who were EGOT winners. You know EGOT is an acronym that stands for the Emmy, Grammy, Oscar, and Tony awards, don't you?"

"I do. I am now impressed that your knowledge has grown so much so quickly," I said smiling as big as possible.

"I now have a purpose. I want to join that select group. Now, can we get started? I think even you will be impressed with my improvement. Of course, I still plan to be humble in my winning and to always appreciate those less fortunate that are not coached by you!" he said, standing to perform as a new person.

Stephen won first place at the next local tournament. He won several invitational tournaments. He, however, placed second at the national qualifying tournament because he went over the ten-minute time limit by thirty seconds. He went to the state finals in Program Reading.

He developed a plan of action he hoped would

result in becoming a professional actor that one day would result in him being the recipient of the EGOT.

When I broke my collarbone playing baseball in a charity game, Stephen came each day in his Rolls Royce and picked me up because I could not drive my stick shift Nova.

Eventually, Stephen performed a cutting from the *Muppets* that won first place in the state in Program Reading. Right after that tournament, Stephen confessed to me he had prerecorded the fake pre-class announcement and played it while Miss Donovan was putting her lunch away in another room.

CHAPTER TWENTY: FRESNO CHRISTIAN ACADEMY

Fresno Christian Academy School

Fresno Chrisitan Academy school was a very special place for many students and faculty members. The faculty were not being paid what they could have earned in the public sector, but for each one, teaching was a ministry for them. Susan, Darla, Carla, and Stephen all benefited from this educational institution. Their lives had been changed forever. They each had a new and improved self-worth, confidence, and respected rules and regulations that governed society.

Unfortunately, Senior Pastor, Reverend John Spencer, made what became known as the "Milliondollar" accounting error in December that caused staff and faculty checks to bounce, and forced an immediate closing of the church and school during the Christmas break. He withdrew church and school funds in the amount of over one million dollars. He left town never to be held accountable for his actions.

I personally was among those who had given so much to the school because I believed we were making a difference and I wanted to be a part of that movement. I experienced what it is like to have the check you depend on to meet financial obligations vanish. It was humiliating to call my credit card companies, my landlord, and especially my sister whom I was helping attend college and let them all know what happened as I tried to make good that which I could not!

News about Fresno Christian Academy spread quickly regarding the financial insolvency of the corporation. An emergency meeting with Principal Hansen and ten parent groups tried to save the school by pledging $100,000 each to reopen it. Litigation prevented that from happening. The pastor was gone, the bank accounts were empty, and a bankruptcy procedure had started prior to the meeting to save the school. With only two weeks' notice all the students, staff, and faculty were forced to leave their school. Most of the teachers pledged to continue teaching for the next month or so without pay until the school could be saved. It was impossible.

Over six hundred students had to enroll in a new school. All the teachers, staff, and administrators were without jobs. We all were forced to experience a new and undeserved life because of the mishap/deliberately calculated exit of a man who was a wolf among us in sheep's clothing.

I was just thirty-two years old and questioned if I could continue to fight the academic fights on behalf of students whether it be in the classroom or in outside activities. I knew I had done my best but was fearful my best was not good enough. I knew there would be a future, I just did not know in what direction I would turn and what I would do to impact and make society better than it was.

POSTSCRIPT

I was fortunate because Clovis High School, a public school within the county, was looking for a new speech coach midyear. I applied and started teaching there in January. Most were not so lucky.

It is fitting that this memoir ends with the story about Stephen. More than anyone else he shared with me what unconditional love and respect in a teacherstudent relationship felt like. He taught me how to demand excellence while at the same time understanding how home-life and peer pressure affect the total well-being of a teenager.

During summer break, Stephen had a friend who stopped by his house riding a new Harley Davidson and asked him to take it for a ride. Two blocks from his home, a drunk driver hit the motorcycle head on and instantly killed Stephen. His life was and remains an inspiration to those who knew and loved him. My life was changed forever.

Collectively, my students taught me as much, if not more than I taught them. I taught a subject matter, but they taught me about life. I think I am a better person because I met students who were challenging and challenged. Together we faced overwhelming obstacles. We overcame most obstacles together. Occasionally, we faced them separately, but ultimately, we faced them and learned.

In the next installment, *Overcoming All Odds: Four,* the reader will be introduced to some additional amazing students I met at the college level from the 1980's until my retirement from forensics in 2006. These students experienced personal, academic, and financial obstacles. Some were successful and unfortunately, some were not.

I hope my writings continue to inspire you to overcome your own difficulties and to have greater empathy for those who are working hard to surmount theirs. All of us need help along the way. I hope you find the people to help you. I did!

www.ingramcontent.com/pod-product-compliance
Lightning Source LLC
Chambersburg PA
CBHW071746120626
46550CB00002B/685